ISRAEL'S DILEMMAS
Arnon Rieger

Traces the creation of a Palestinian State by Israel's Military Victory in 1967

THIS BOOK IS DEDICATED TO THE MEMORIES OF MY HIGH SCHOOL CLASSMATES,

YAAKOV BUCHMAN

URI ALADJEM

MOSHE HOCHBERG

WHO WERE KILLED IN DEFENSIVE WARS AGAINST THE ARABS

"COMPETING PRESSURES TEMPT ONE TO BELIEVE THAT AN ISSUE DEFFERD IS A PROBLEM AVOIDED; MORE OFTEN IT IS A CRISIS INVENTED"- HENRY KISSINGER

CONTENTS

Preface

The Arab-Israeli conflict has surpassed all other international issues in its durability and intractability. It has generated the most intense partisanship even among people far from the region and unfamiliar with its complexities— and this intractability is borne out by the writing that comes from the troubled region.

This book is designed to fill a gap in the literature regarding the Arab-Israeli conflict by unwinding these complexities. An enormous amount has been written about this conflict, but none of these works have penetrated the fundamental issues that lie behind it.

The reader, in trying to find something that will provide a useful background and explanation regarding the conflict, searches in vain for a serious account. I decided to write this book because I believe that Israel stands at a crossroads. The course Israel chooses will not just affect the tenor of its life as a nation, but will also determine whether or not it can continue to exist.

Both scholarly and popular discussions are often limited to the current diplomatic maneuvers. The conflict is usually understood as an Israeli-Palestinian problem, which is, in my opinion, a digression. This conflict was initiated by the entire Arab world and has to be solved with the entire Arab world. Israeli occupation of Palestinian lands took place in a war of self-defense in 1967 against the entire Arab world. Omission of the entire Arab world as a partner for solving the Palestinian problem is making its resolution impossible.

It must be noted that self -serving political considerations of the United States, and those of Europe, often camouflage the real problems in the Middle East since Israel tends to cave in under diplomatic pressures—more so than the Arabs.

What the reader will find in this book is neither an emotional religious/biblical approach to Israel's problems nor a human rights angle on the current dispute, but simply a systematic, logical approach to the current conflict.

I would like to thank my wife Diane, the Falmouth Writer's Group, and Marlene Bell, who offered me her editorial skills without financial compensation. Thanks are also due to Marvin Lechten and Kenneth Brown for their useful comments. Without them this book would not have seen the light of day.

Prologue

Israel's destiny is inextricably tied to U.S. policy in the Middle East region. The United States is practically the sole provider of Israel's military assistance and to a lesser degree its economic assistance. Without U.S. support, the existence of the Jewish state is in doubt. Therefore, whenever we discuss Israel's present behaviors we have to evaluate and review them against the U.S. foreign policy at large and the diplomatic and military exercise options the United States practices in the Middle East in particular.

The United States finds itself with a new and difficult task; it is constantly searching for what its purpose should be in a world that is constantly changing. Although the Cold War from 1945 to 1992 held many disturbing threats to U.S. interests and survival, at the same time it provided the United States a certainty of purpose and a measure of planning coherence. The United States is the only superpower in a world that is growing steadily more diverse, a world in which U.S. power is increasingly ill fitted to deal with these problems. Past U.S. National leadership administrations were accustomed to dealing with other national leaderships with well-established structured governments; the political actors who shaped the world were rational actors, if not necessarily moral or decent. Today it is more difficult to deal with shadowy players who do not lead national governments—groups that very much act irrationally and leave no room for negotiation.

The end of the Cold War, in 1992, accelerated political movements for self-determination, led by many of the world's ethnic and religious groups seeking a country of their own. However, many of the new governments were not up to the task of governing. Through either mismanagement or malice, some of these governments have made the lives of their citizens miserable. Some of these countries created a culture out of politics and economic despair to spawn the growth of informal and illegal economies, particularly the rapid expansion of major criminal organizations. These organizations further undermined the stability of many of the world's fledgling countries. The international community was put in a position to rescue failed countries such as Yugoslavia, Rwanda, Somalia, and others.

It is in this environment that a democratic superpower such as the United States must find its way. In the new order of challenges, most do not present themselves with the apparent clarity of the Cold War. Therefore, they impose a great deal more on U.S. Leadership. Leadership inevitably involves an element of faith; to act in anticipation of events it is required that followers believe the rationale they are given before events manifest themselves with all their consequences.

Leadership has to overcome not only external pressures, but internal ones as well, such as various government agencies, the legislature, and the public at large in its offshoot of lobbyist groups. A true leader has to have the will, the stamina, and the understanding to deal wisely with many complex and often ambiguous circumstances in order to implement his or her policy. However, in a democracy, no policy, regardless of how well it is conceived, is worth much if it cannot engender public support. This is the crux of the matter: How do you get a truly informed public? Are the leaders better off with an uninformed public so they can manipulate the public through clever propaganda or the mass media (as it is called today since "propaganda" has a negative connotation)?

The public receives its information from the mass media, which the experts call the fourth estate. To an outsider, the proliferation of media communication sources that bombard the public 24 hours per day, seven days a week—with instant analysis by political pundits who have instant solutions for every problem—should signal that the public is well informed. Certainly the floods of facts support this assumption. The sad reality is that the abundance of facts does not enhance our understanding of a specific situation. In many cases, it is inadvertently actually the cause of our diminished understanding. There is a saying that in the past, philosophers and scientists knew a little bit about a large number of subjects. As time progressed, they knew more and more about fewer and fewer subjects; thus the time would come, in the future, when they would have an infinite knowledge about nothing. We are now in this advanced stage when it comes to understanding real political maneuvers in both the domestic and foreign arenas.

The real source for making sense out of the multitude of facts has to be the media, both the written and the visual. After all, excluding the tabloids, the media as our fourth estate is independent of the three government branches. However, with commercialization and the fierce competitiveness between the various media moguls for the largest audience, the trend today is toward tabloidism, gossipism, and flashy reporting rather than the true conviction of intellectual honesty. The race to be the first to get a scoop is what determines journalistic success. The major issues of the day are being discussed with quick sound bites and catchy phrases. Everybody has to join one of the political camps, that is, conservative, neo-conservative, or liberal. Labeling an individual as a proponent of any of these movements automatically defines him or her, with no more need to elaborate further on any specific issue. Dialogue or discussion is nothing more than a series of monologues. The old art of debate is transformed into a shouting match. The collapse of Communism and the triumph of capitalism could have signaled the end of ideology. Not so fast, say the media mavens—we all subscribe to the conspiracy theory that the liberals are about to take over the media and crush the other point of view (or that the conservatives are). President Bush can do no wrong according to the conservatives and do no right according to the liberals. The same applied to President Clinton, except in reverse. Political parties developed a feeling of beleaguered paranoia, and they hold frequent conventions to rally their troops with slogan-style emotionally charged speeches.

These emotional attitudes toward any political issue create immunity from understanding the real problem and an inability to discuss it on its own merits. The opposition to the Vietnam War was based on a prolonged conflict with heavy casualties and constant appalling images on the TV screen. The question whether or not the United States should be involved in Vietnam in the first place was raised by only a very few at the beginning of the U.S. Involvement. As the war dragged on, the questioning became a loud chorus. Had the United States won the war in Vietnam shortly after the French left, this would have been another success for the progressive United States against the evil Soviet empire. Similarly, the first Gulf War in 1991 was hailed as the crowning achievement for Bush senior's administration only because of its shorter duration and fewer casualties. Very few people questioned why there was a need for the U.S. intervention while the regional countries that were threatened by Saddam Hussein should and could evict him themselves from Kuwait but were unwilling to. After all, even Iran would have been eager to join such a coalition.

11

In the second Gulf War, the patriotic
cheerleading of the press and the vast majority
of the public at large reached a fevered pitch
only because of the lightning military victory
with few casualties, drowning out the
necessary critical and skeptical component that
would ask why invade Iraq? The war with Iraq
was based on false premises and was sold via
misleading of the public at large. After all, Iraq
did not threaten the United States with
weapons of mass destruction (WMD); neither
did it support Al Qaeda overtly. The fact that
Saddam was a brutal, tyrannical leader implies
that the United States must make the same
effort in Saudi Arabia, Iran, North Korea, Libya,
Sudan, and many other countries in Asia,
South America, and Africa. The reason for the
Iraqi invasion can be attributed to a colossal
incompetence and cover-up of the real issue
facing the United States. The invasion had
nothing to do with the war on terrorism but
simply showed that the president was taking
action. Iraq was targeted because it made a
mistake by invading Kuwait, a country that
produces oil. The United States evicted the
Iraqis from Kuwait with the full support of the
UN. Following the military defeat, the UN
imposed sanctions on Iraq to force it to dispose
of its WMD. This made Iraq a vulnerable state
in the eyes of the international community.
When George W. Bush was faced with the
need for action in the aftermath of 9/11/01, as
an opportunist he picked Iraq after
Afghanistan, since he had failed to capture Al
Qaeda in Tora Bora and had had minimal
success in controlling Pakistan's nuclear

proliferation to the terrorists. Saddam Hussein was simply unfortunate to have been vulnerable at the wrong time.

The cheerleaders for the American victory in Iraq should have come back to earth once they remembered that it took Israel only six days to defeat a combined force of Egyptians, Syrians, Iraqis, Jordanians, and Saudis without precision bombing and high-tech weaponry and with half the troops. The Arab armies are nothing more than a reflection of their own societies. The fact that cowardly global terrorism appears in Arab society is directly related to its own societal backwardness and the lack of professionalism in its armed forces. Past U.S. victories such as those in the first Gulf War and Afghanistan should not mislead the Pentagon, because the ghost of Vietnam can reappear to haunt them if they attempt preemptive actions against non-Muslim countries such as North Korea. It is abundantly clear to the U.S. skippers that the United States' preeminence as a military power in the world cannot sustain the same course as displayed in Iraq and reinforce its status in the world as the new Rome, ready and willing to subdue the barbarian hordes. In the first place, the public will not support such adventures. Economically, such a course would be a disaster, and politically it would isolate the United States in the international community.

The United States will not abandon its consensus in supporting international institutions, such as the UN, despite its unilateralist action against Iraq. However, a wiser and more effective way of using its military power would be to use diplomatic pressure. This pressure will keep the world order without the actual use of military might, but only as a background, as during the Cold War. Iraq's invasion of Kuwait might not have happened had the U.S. ambassador to Iraq called Saddam and warned him of the consequences of such an invasion. The same could have applied to Al Qaeda terrorist actions prior to 9/11/01 if all the Arab states and Afghanistan had been warned as to the seriousness of these actions. Unfortunately, the United States has not displayed a coherent foreign policy in the past. Rather than leadership obviating the need for military action, U.S. vacillation and inconsistency have brought about military actions as a substitute for leadership. Fireworks replace thoughtful policy and simply show that one is doing something.

Neither the Western world's leadership, nor its press, is willing to confront the real issues of fighting terrorism. The Arab states constitute a monolithic entity. These "nation states" were created by the British Empire as a result of the defeat of the Ottoman Empire in World War I and were based on payoffs to the various sheiks that had supported Britain's military campaign against the Ottoman Empire. The Arabs with their Islamic philosophy are the only ethnic and religious group that is active in *global* terrorism. The many other groups involved in terrorism limit their activities to their own countries and have known political agendas, however fanatical and irrational this sounds to outsiders and insiders. Again, the Arabs are the only group that poses a threat on a global level and manages to intimidate and confuse the Western world. The West shows ambivalence in its reaction to this menace by increasing security within and exerting its full military force, as in Afghanistan and Iraq, and then kowtowing to the rest of the Arab world. The West fails to realize, perhaps because of diplomatic and tactical expediency, that all Arab Middle East countries, overtly or covertly, support all the terrorist groups as long as they themselves are not subjected to terrorism.

The differentiation between the various terrorist groups belongs within the academic world and not within the political arena. All the Arab terrorist groups get their inspiration from the Koran, and they view Israel and the United States as Western powers that intend to occupy their Holy Land. They all use the same tactic of terrorizing the civilian population in the hope of restoring an Islamic caliphate. None of them are open for negotiations. The only difference between the various terrorist groups is the geographic location of their activities and their local commanders. The Palestinian Liberation Organization (PLO) is a terrorist organization like all the others.

At the end of the Middle Ages, in the 15Th century, Europeans saw social reforms that brought them an ever-improving political and economic way of life. The feudalistic society was replaced eventually with free enterprise, and clerical authority was replaced by civil rights with political institutions.

The Far East saw major social and economic reforms only in the 20th century, and these countries have the fastest-growing economies in the world. Only the Arabs remain, even today, a feudalistic, autocratic, corrupt tribal society. Many scholars have made attempts to explain this phenomenon of a lack of reform in Arab society over more than 600 years. This stagnation persists despite these countries' huge oil reserves and revenues; their GDPs, excluding oil revenue, remain lower than that of Albania, which is the poorest country in Europe. Oil became the curse of the industrial countries; oil is energy, energy is money, money is control, and control is power that can be used to benefit society. However, oil in the wrong hands is money misspent and control corrupted. Control corrupted is power abused, and power abused is force misused in its various forms, which leads to worldwide terrorism. With oil out of the control of the Arab tyrants, global terrorism would die. Diplomatic initiatives to boycott industrial support and importation of Arab oil, and/or blocking their ports of exit, would starve the terrorists for cash and they would fade away without a whimper.

No outside military power will bring about democracy or any other social changes to Arab society. The Arabs have to do it themselves, as happened in Europe and the Far East without the oil. The Arabs have to understand that they themselves must bear the responsibility for any action by their people in global terrorism that leads to the above-recommended diplomatic and military actions. It is very important to send a clear message that the Arabs will understand—the West will leave them alone and they should leave the West alone. Once they plunge back into their medieval tribal way of life, as is being recommended by Al Qaeda and other Muslim fundamentalists, they will realize how backward they are and may pay more attention to their own social reforms. The policy of live and let live is far better than the present one of misleading and confusing, which is heading nowhere and only prolongs this confrontation.

The present confrontation between a Western opportunist leadership that uses the mass media to disseminate misinformation and perhaps even uses infomercial tactics in its diplomatic maneuvers, on the one hand, and a single-minded virulent Muslim world will not be solved soon. Even when they exercise their military option, the United States and the rest of the Western world do not bring it to its conclusion, but always end up in some sort of mediation that prolongs the crisis. To suppose that those trapped by intellectual poverty are actually incapable of democracy smacks of racism pure and simple. Thus Western actors constantly argue and apologize excessively for their pure moral and philanthropic intentions in pursuing their military actions. They never want their actions to be viewed as a self-serving, prolonged occupation, but only, as in the case of the wars in Afghanistan and Iraq, as a means for the betterment of the people in order to liberate them from a brutal regime. This is classic diplomatic self-indulgence in the name of noblesse oblige. The Western leaders want to get credit for the noblesse and force Israel to pay the cost of oblige by creating a Palestinian state.

Many respectable European pundits display their old form of anti-Semitic feelings not against the Arabs, who raised havoc in the West with terrorist acts, but against the Jews. Articles in the respectable press have suggested that a group of 20 people who took their places in the Bush administration, hoping to overthrow Saddam Hussein and spread American ideas of democracy throughout the Middle East, are neo-conservative Jews. Not only do these Jews have protection of Israel on their agenda, but also, according to a member of the French parliament (quoting his country's foreign minister, Dominique de Villepin), "The hawks in the US administration are in the hands of Ariel Sharon." This after Israel gave the Sinai to Egypt without a real peace, and with the "road map" for a Palestinian state in place despite the continuous terror in Israel. This reinforces the dictum that anti-Semitism does not emanate from the strength of its victim but from its weakness.

In this chaotic world, Israel finds itself residing in the midst of a volatile Muslim region with a misconstrued U.S. diplomatic policy, keeps its

18

silence with no protest and the forcing of diplomatic confrontation, and has allowed itself to be totally manipulated by the big powers even when its future survival is at stake. Israel is unable to counter the Arabs' constant insistence on linking any issue involving Arab misbehaviors with the Arab-Israeli conflict. The world communities at large, and the United States, are supporting this linkage in particular. Can Israel survive under such conditions and with inept leadership and polity? What does Israel have to do to survive? That is the subject of this book.

Introduction

In my humble opinion, the Arab-Israeli dispute started in November 1947, when the UN partition plan created the Jewish State of Israel. This conflict can therefore "celebrate" close to 60 years, making it one of the longest unabated conflicts in the history of international relations. Many pundits claim that the end of the conflict is very near—all that is required is for the United States to pressure Israel enough for Israel to meet the Palestinians' full aspirations. But the language that is being used by the international community, including the United States, of "submission to the Arab pressures" and "declaring victory via supremacy," is Orwellian.

Shortsightedness will only aggravate the situation in the Middle East.

It is true that without the existence of the State of Israel, the conflict would not exist, but the absence of a Jewish state would not necessarily have meant the existence of a Palestinian state.

The present situation can be traced to 1967. On May 15 of that year, Abdul Nasser—the leader of the UAR (United Arab Republic, which included Egypt and Syria)—made both political and military moves to annihilate the Jewish state. These moves were made because of the urging of the Soviet Union. Nasser blocked the Suez Canal and the Straits of Tiran to Israeli ships, ordered the UN forces from Sinai where they'd been stationed since 1956, moved his troops to Sinai, and moved Syrian troops to the Golan Heights in a clear posture of invading and destroying Israel. None of the superpowers was prepared to defuse the situation. France with its "moral" leader Charles De Gaulle wanted out of North Africa; and the United States, in a deep quagmire in Vietnam, ignored the situation completely, despite the fact that an Arab victory would have resulted in deeper penetration of the Soviet Union into the Middle East and the elimination of a capitalist state (Israel) from the world map. All the Western leaders were unified in urging Israel not to initiate a preemptive strike. Israel found itself and its entire economy in a standstill. Its entire citizen army was stationed at the borders.

Fast-forward three weeks . . .

Between the 5th and 10th of June 1967, Israel defied world opinion and acted preemptively. Soon, the Egyptian and Syrian armies had been destroyed, and Israel had control of Sinai, the Golan Heights, the West Bank, and the Gaza Strip. Now, as if waking up from hibernation, the entire world—through the UN and the superpowers—found itself involved in furious diplomatic activities.

Israel gave up the uninhabited area of the Sinai and kept the inhabited land that the resident Arabs now want as a Palestinian state.

The reason for the conquest of these territories was to prevent the annihilation of the State of Israel. It was not to oppress the Palestinians. The Palestinian problem is thus a result of the Arab states' aggression against Israel, and these states should therefore be part of the solution.

Admiral Hyman G. Rickover once said, "Great minds discuss ideas, average minds discuss events, small minds discuss people." Many well-meaning "average-mind" "experts" who covered the Arab-Israeli conflict of 1967 have chronicled the forces and the facts behind the events. They filled up volumes of best-sellers, but the reality was stated best by UAR leader Nasser himself in his "resignation" speech on 23 July 1967 when he said that his actions were purely defensive measures, necessary to help Syria under the new treaty—that as well as a matter of honor and solidarity, the question was also one of Egypt's own security. But earlier, on May 26, in a speech to the Arab trade unionists, when things seemed to be going his way, Nasser had described the sequence of events in a different light:

> We were waiting for the day when we would be fully prepared . . . I say nothing aimlessly. One day, two years ago, I stood up to say that we have no plan to

*liberate Palestine . . . recently we
felt we are strong enough, that if
we were to enter a battle, with
God's help we could triumph . . .*

To a "great mind" as defined by Admiral Rickover, the issue is, pure and simple, eradication of Israel.

If we were to draw an analogy to the present situation between Israel and the Arabs, we could use the end of World War II. The Nazis' original claim was to liberate the German ethnic group in Czechoslovakia and Poland. The victorious powers would request both Czechoslovakia and Poland to establish autonomous states to include the ethnic Germans. Instead, Poland occupied Prussia after the Soviet Union "converted" Eastern Poland into West Ukraine; and those Germans, 12 to 15 million, who had lived in these territories for centuries were expelled from the territories and became refugees in Germany. They were absorbed and the issue was not prolonged. The lesson that was applied to Germany is a simple one: You pay the consequences of losing a war that you initiated, there is no going back. However, this lesson cannot be applied to the Arabs, because Israel with its five million people is not a major player in the international arena and the Arabs have oil and 300 million people.

The current Israeli economic and security crisis cannot be understood and brought under control without a rethinking of the present course of Israel's foreign policy. Central to this crisis is the ever-increasing dependency of Israel on U.S. financial and military support without U.S. political and diplomatic support. This dependency brings Israel, dangerously, toward a large-scale catastrophe since it delays further and further, to the point of no perceived future, the possibility of ever achieving a true peace treaty with its Arab neighbors. This economic dependency allowed the U.S. foreign policy in the Middle East to transform Israel's military might into an ineffective force as a diplomatic tool for achieving Israel's desire to live in peace with its neighbors. This book is an attempt to explain how Israel was brought to this juncture in its history, which may seal its demise.

Without being overly pretentious, I would like to set my approach to the subject with two famous quotes from Andre Gide that have guided me since my early life:

> What another would have done
> as well as you, do not do it. What
> another would have said as well
> do not write it. Be faithful to that
> which exists nowhere but
> yourself—and thus make
> yourself.

> A unanimous chorus of praise is
> not an assurance of survival;
> authors who please everyone at
> once are quickly exhausted. I
> would prefer to think that

hundreds years hence people will
say we did not properly
understand [an author].

I was born in Eretz Yisrael in what the rest of
the world called Palestine. I was nine years old
when the State of Israel was declared, to the
delight of world Jewry. It was the culmination of
a 2,000-year dream. It almost put an end to the
argument, by various factions, within the
various Jewish groups as to whether Judaism
is a religion or a nationality. The creation of
Israel united the Orthodoxy and Reform in
support of Zionism.

Though I am now an American citizen, I
consider the country in question to be my own
country. I do not write as a dispassionate
observer. I write with the hope that this
analysis will rouse writers and politicians from
their torpor. My intention is to alert them to the
catastrophe that can befall the future of the
country, and to inspire them to take the difficult
steps to transform their thinking to a more
critical attitude toward the polity and the
leadership quality of Israel. If we do not seize
this opportunity to change our critical view of
Israeli behavior, by the time the truth sinks in it
may well be too late to act.

I witnessed the War of Independence (1948-
49), the Sinai Campaign (1956, in which I
actively participated), the Six-Day War (1967),
and the Yom Kippur War (1973)—the last two
as a U.S. resident. These last two wars,
although ending with an Israeli military triumph,

25

resulted in a total geopolitical disaster and threaten to reverse Israel's fortune into the possibility of its complete demise.

Israel was allowed to keep the occupied territories, for reasons that I will review later on, without any major pressures from the great powers, in particular the one that counts most, the United States. As I visited Israel frequently and read the enormous volume of articles and books that analyzed the aftermath of the Six-Day War, it was clear to me that all of them (ignoring the transparently anti-Israeli works) dealt in ideological polemics. They never touched on the lack of a clear-cut Israeli official strategic policy regarding the new reality resulting from the aftermath of the war.

Immediately after the wars there were some articles and books, by a wide spectrum of Israeli political parties, with specific executable plans that urged the government to act, but these plans were neither adopted nor even brought up for discussion by the government. The Israeli leadership simply took the line of least resistance, which was to do nothing, and declared to the whole world that for a "final peace" everything was negotiable. This "policy" was feasible as long as the Arabs refused to negotiate with Israel. It came apart with the Yom Kippur War in 1973 and completely collapsed with Sadat's visit to Israel in 1977. This should have been glaring evidence, to anybody who was Israel's friend, of the failure of Israel's impotent leadership throughout its entire political spectrum. The leaders did not

26

rise to the occasion to reap geopolitical fruits from a magnificent military victory in a war that they had not sought and that had been imposed upon them.

On many occasions, I wrote letters to the editor attempting to remind readers and writers that the Israeli government was participating in a strange diplomatic game that could be understood only by psychologists. None of my letters were published. I finally resorted to writing directly to the authors of the articles and received interesting short responses. Their responses can be summed up, in general terms, as follows: "Your comments are very interesting [i.e., you don't know what you're talking about], and the Israeli government has enough troubles without piling on it accusations of incompetence."

I then noticed in the Western press that the mainstream journalists and columnists never use, when describing politicians, adjectives such as incapable, moronic, incompetent, or useless. They will not even, in a more polite style, say that the political activists are afraid to face reality and to make tough decisions. They are always trying to "explain" the politicians' moves as if they were based on ideological and/or other forces (external or internal). In this manner, the writer does not insult any individual and thus can always retain his or her privileges to access the politician in the future. Furthermore, most journalists, whether they are reporters or columnists, relate to the diplomatic moves of past events within a time span of only a few months. I approached an academician after her lengthy lecture on the Palestinian-Israeli conflict with a question as to what the Six-Day War was all about and asked her if she had ever noticed in history examples in which the aggressor, after being defeated in the battlefield, came out in a better geopolitical position. She gave me a lengthy dissertation to the effect that in today's world things are different from what they were 40 years ago.

In the affluent, enlightened, and liberal Western world where status quo is the prevailing modus operandi and where no major upheavals endanger society, the above-mentioned civility of journalism is an accepted mode. The mass media is part of entertainment and not a political force for change. We are accustomed to providing rhetoric and discussion, in public, on almost any issue and providing background for a civilized debate. We do this even if the main purpose of the advocate is to inflame emotions and the message is not a legitimate one and, by our standards, is an affront to civilized discourse and not deserving of attention. The press is full of coverage of any political issue only on the superficial level and how it is reflected by a specific personality. The coverage is full of irrelevant details and obscures the real, significant forces and the ways in which they interrelate to the main issue. These forms of clutter information prevent the average citizen from understanding the issues at hand. Very few writers in the media establishment are beacons of clear thought amid a sea of "mushiness." Most serve the existing institutions and the politicians in office in their desire to avoid the tough decisions and allow their lobbyists to operate undisturbed so that they can stay in power without fear of being replaced. However, when it comes to Israel, the "civility" of not dealing with more unsparing candor and commonsense insight, directly, openly, and honestly, with the real issues in the Middle East is crucially counterproductive. It is mandatory and essential, in order to prevent Israel from incurring ultimate destruction, to discuss these issues without any inhibitions and without concern for style, form, or political correctness.

There are very few facts in this book that the well-versed reader will not already know from other published articles and books. This work takes the form of an anthology of many ideas by different authors as presented in books, articles, and newspaper editorials. None of these authors have arrived at the inevitable conclusion that I have formed here, which is my main intention for this writing. I explain this conclusion by using several unbiased, cohesive, and coherent vantage points relating to the present political situation in which Israel is embroiled.

My background is neither journalistic nor academic in the area of political science; however, I felt obliged to write this work out of my own frustration in communicating with the media at large and the Israeli media in particular. I have never belonged to a circle or clique; mine is simply the opinion of a minority of one. Not being part of the media or the journalistic establishment, I do not need to disguise my views, however unpalatable they will be to some. I attempt here to provide a systematic and rational approach to the Arab-Israeli conflict in its historical perspective and to delineate where we are now and why the future of Israel may be doomed. I will provide evidence indicating why Israel is sliding into the abyss and suggest that its destruction cannot be averted unless some radical changes take place. I will pinpoint the historical events in which true leadership was displayed and those in which leadership glaringly failed, and why. The history of the Jews as it relates to the Middle East is important, as is the Arabs' behavior, if one is to see in perspective how and why Israel is moving in the direction of the abyss.

I hope that this essay will encourage others to expound and expand more articulately on what I have written. The intent is to stimulate exposure by more credible writers so that the discussion can reach a wider audience and bear political activism with positive results in Israel, in particular, and the world of the Jewish community at large.

A Short History of Zionism

In 1960, I visited Europe after completing my compulsory military service. Most of my time was spent in the United Kingdom since I have relatives there. In one of my visits to Cambridge or Oxford, I read in the university bulletin that there would be a debate on the topic "Were the Super Powers Correct in Establishing the State of Israel?" The exact wording of the topic and the debate's location are based on my memory and could be inaccurate; however, that accuracy is not relevant to my point here. I went to the debate and saw that the Jewish students defended the superpower actions toward establishing the State of Israel. Then a non-Jewish female student argued fiercely that Israel was created not by the superpowers, but by its own people who settled and toiled on the land and thus were entitled to their own country. Her argument taught me a valuable lesson in the art of debate. By defining the issue through the topic, the Arab students, who had organized this debate, forced the Israeli supporters to admit that Israel was an outside invasive entity supported by outside superpowers and thus, according to the Arab propaganda, that its fate would follow the fate of the Crusaders. The Jewish students, who accepted that formulation of the topic, would have lost the debate had it not been for the non-Jewish student who was able to get to the bottom of the issue and saved the day.

The reality is more complex than it first seems. It did involve limited intervention from a reluctant superpower. But for the most part, Jewish leadership in Europe and the United States and great masses of Jewish pioneers settled, at great sacrifice, Eretz Yisrael.

Although there has always been a small Jewish presence in what is now Israel, most Jews were forced to leave the Middle East after the failed uprisings against the Romans in 69 and 135 C.E. The Jews in the Diaspora survived, for the most part in Europe, for almost two millennia under their religious orthodox way of life. Despite their constant persecution and the pressure to convert, they never considered the option of returning to Zion. There was one known case in 1211, when 300 rabbis and their students from France and England settled in Eretz Yisrael. Although this impressed many Jews, it turned into a fiasco when all of the settlers returned to Europe after a few years. They were unable to survive on merely studying Torah without at the same time providing themselves with food. One cannot claim that the Jews of the Middle Ages were lacking in courage, since they were willing to die by fire as martyrs rather than convert. Their minds were concentrated on a religious rather than a political Zionism.

It was only toward the end of the 19th century that a modern political Zionist movement was established in Russia; it was called "Lovers of Zion." The "First Immigration Wave" that started in 1882 and the "Second Immigration

Wave" that started in 1904 were both the result of the movement of the Lovers of Zion. This immigration and all the others were a direct result of the distress and hardship the Jews suffered in Eastern Europe through the relentless pogroms. During the same period, between 1882 and 1914, the world saw the largest migration of Jews to the United States, in excess of 2,000,000, while only 40,000 immigrated to Eretz Yisrael.

The "Third Immigration Wave," which started at the end of First World War, was already more organized after the establishment of the political Zionist movement under the leadership of Theodore Herzl. Eretz Yisrael was then under British rule. On July 24, 1922, Britain received from the League of Nations an official mandate to rule over Palestine.

The first well-concentrated and organized effort to solve the Jewish problem of Europe can be attributed to Theodore Herzl. He organized the political Zionist movement after concluding that the Jews must leave the land of their dispersion and be concentrated in a sovereign state. The Zionist leadership always understood that the European powers would be willing partners in this effort, since it would be to their benefit as well.

The opportunity presented itself during the First World War when the British and the French were about to defeat the Ottoman Empire in the Middle East. Chaim Weizmann, who had migrated to Britain from Russia in 1904 and was active in the Zionist movement, was instrumental in getting a commitment from the British government in the form of a letter to Lord Rothchild from the foreign secretary, Arthur Balfour. This became known as the Balfour Declaration of November 2, 1917. The commitment made in the Balfour Declaration was that after the conquest of Palestine, for the first time, the British government would support the establishment of a Jewish Homeland in Palestine.

Many historians explain the Balfour Declaration in terms of Britain's imperial self-interests. According to these historians, since the British were in competition with the French over influence in the Middle East, by allying themselves with the Jews they could secure control of Palestine. However, this does not explain the fact that the same territory was promised to the Arabs within the framework of the McMahon-Hussein correspondence of 1915-16. Via this correspondence, Britain undertook to support the establishment of an independent Arab state in return for an Arab revolt against the Ottoman Empire. A more plausible explanation is that the Balfour Declaration resulted from the influence and the tenacity of the Zionist leadership in Britain and, foremost, the influence of Chaim Weizmann. He took a gamble on Britain's defeating the Ottoman Empire and was successful in convincing the British that the Jews would be a formidable ally of Britain. What helped him was the fact that Arab nationalism was in its infancy. Furthermore, the Dreyfus Affair and the plight of the Eastern European Jews, who were being subjected to one pogrom after another, horrified Europe and forced Britain to find a way out of this situation.

So successful was the Zionist leadership that under the League of Nations system of mandates that Britain undertook, on July 24, 1922 the mandate of Palestine incorporated the Balfour Declaration and recognized the Jewish community on the West Bank of the Jordan River. This prevented the submission to the Arabs of all the territory west of the Jordan as had been promised to them under the framework of the McMahon-Hussein correspondence of 1915-16.

Although the Jewish and the Arab communities lived side by side without being represented in the mandatory government, which was run through the colonial offices in London, the arrangement allowed time for the Jewish community to increase their population in Eretz Yisrael and strengthen their institutions for future negotiations.

Chaim Weizmann understood the importance of the Yishuv (the Jewish settlement in Eretz Yisrael) as a force for future autonomy; however, at the same time he recognized the importance of British cooperation in allowing the Yishuv to grow before future autonomy could be achieved.

This view could not be taken for granted, though, since Zeev Jabotinsky (1880-1940) felt differently. He was a contemporary of Chaim Weizmann and Weizmann's partner in the leadership of the Zionist movement. Jabotinsky advocated a mobilization of the European Jews within the framework of the British army to conquer Eretz Yisrael on both sides of the Jordan River to create a Jewish state. He regarded a slow buildup of the Yishuv in Eretz Yisrael as counterproductive, believing that it would expose the settlers to Arab resistance without credible Jewish military protection. He managed to establish three battalions as the "Jewish Legion" under his command and participated in the defense of the City of Jerusalem in April 1920 against the Arab riots. Jabotinsky was so convinced that Britain would support his idea to its ultimate goal and retain the Jewish Legion permanently, that he refused to budge even when the British issued their "White Papers" to limit Jewish immigration to Eretz Yisrael.

Chaim Weizmann faced the reality of Britain's caving in to Arab pressures and thus supported a policy of aggressive settlement with the establishment of supporting institutions. This change in tactics—from seeking British support to relying on the establishment of the Yishuv—was paramount in achieving the Jewish Homeland with or without British support.

The first Arab riot in Jerusalem, in 1920, was crushed by Britain when the Yishuv numbered close to 85,000 Jews, which constituted less than 12% of the total population. This forced the Jewish authorities in Eretz Yisrael to establish the Hagana or Jewish Defense Force. From then on, any Arab riot was faced with Jewish resistance, to the displeasure of the British authorities. However, as Arab riots increased in frequency and ferocity, the British succumbed to Arab pressure to avoid the increase of the Jewish population in Eretz Yisrael. The British did this through their policy of not cooperating with the Jewish Agency, which was the semi-official Jewish government, and by issuing the White Papers.

The White Papers were a special implementation policy decree, and their main intention was to limit the Jewish immigration to Eretz Yisrael and to guarantee an Arab majority in Eretz Yisrael. Britain issued White Papers in 1922, 1931, and 1939, each one under pressure from the Arabs, while the situation of the Jews in Europe was desperate. In 1931, it was the German Jews who were fleeing; and in 1939, again during the Second World War, Eastern European Jewry was under physical threat. It was abundantly clear that Britain was siding with the Arabs. After the Peel Commission (established in 1936) recommended the partition of Eretz Yisrael in July 1937, which was accepted by Jews and rejected by Arabs, Britain ignored its mandate totally and supported an Arab state in Eretz Yisrael. The White Paper of 1939 provided for the eventual creation of an Arab-dominated Palestinian state after 10 years and limited Jewish immigration to 75,000 over the next five years, with any future Jewish entry depending on Arab acquiescence. All this while the sheer survival of the Jews in Europe, trapped under Hitler, was doomed and the Jews were unable to enter Eretz Yisrael.

At this juncture of history, it was clear that Britain could no longer be regarded as a partner to the Zionists' enterprise. This brought about the ascendancy of the Yishuv leadership and replaced the traditional Diaspora leaders, such as Chaim Weizmann and Zeev Jabotinsky, with David Ben Gurion, who emerged as a prominent leader. Ben Gurion's colleagues in the Zionist movement believed that the Zionist program would lead to unlimited Jewish immigration to Eretz Yisrael and the creation of a Jewish Homeland under the British protectorate. Ben Gurion believed that, with Britain retracting from its original pledge to the Zionists, the creation of a full-fledged Jewish state was feasible and not a dream. In the midst of the Second World War, when the fate of the European Jews was known, Ben Gurion sought to replace Britain as a sponsor of the Jewish state with the United States; however, he met with a cold shoulder from President Roosevelt. He then initiated the Biltmore Program, a resolution adopted by an extraordinary Zionist conference that took place at the Biltmore Hotel in New York in May 1942. The resolution called for the establishment of a Jewish Commonwealth in Palestine to be integrated into the structure of the new democratic world.

This created for the first time a Jewish political lobby in the United States, where the majority of the Jewish population lived, toward establishing a Jewish state. At the end of the Second World War, when the magnitude of the disaster to the European Jews was revealed and over 100,000 displaced people roamed aimlessly, the Hagana tried to smuggle them to Eretz Yisrael while encouraging most of them to march to the American military camps. This, together with political pressure in the United States, was intended to persuade the United States to force Britain to open the blockade in Eretz Yisrael. President Truman attempted to do just that, although to no avail. However, this action convinced Britain, which was bankrupt after the war, in the spring of 1947 to hand its control of Eretz Yisrael back to the UN.

On November 29, 1947, the UN General Assembly voted for the establishment of a Jewish state and an Arab state in Eretz Yisrael. This resolution would never have happened had it not been for the support of the Soviet Union and its new satellite Eastern European countries. The United States supported the resolution reluctantly. Had it not been for the Soviet Union, there would have been no resolution. Historians will argue as to why Andre Gromyko, the Soviet Union UN representative, delivered the most pro-Zionist speech in the UN. Mostly they claim that the Soviet Union was interested in forcing imperial Britain from the Middle East. This argument does not withstand the facts in the field, since Britain was well entrenched in the Arab Middle East through the Arab League, and furthermore, voting against the resolution would simply force the UN to establish an Arab state in Eretz Yisrael. A more plausible explanation is that Stalin, with his anti-Semitic philosophy, exaggerated the influence and the power of the Jews in the United States. He was hoping that by supporting a Jewish state, the U.S. Jews would prevent the United States from attacking his satellite states in Eastern Europe until such time as he had the atomic bomb. Stalin was also crucial in supplying the new Jewish state with valuable weapons in 1948, during the War of Independence, while the West, led by the United States, imposed a strict embargo on weapons to the new state. In the 1950s, when Stalin had the atomic bomb, the Soviet Union changed its Middle East policy 180 degrees by throwing support to the Arabs.

Prior to and during the War of Independence, Ben Gurion was instrumental in establishing a unified, effective fighting force from a collection of prima donna officers and their own army groups that enabled Israel to beat the Arab states' armies.

In hindsight, we can clearly state that had it not been for the Balfour Declaration, the persecution of the Eastern European Jews, the Arab countries' Jewry, the Holocaust, and the support of the Soviet Union at the crucial moment, there would be no Jewish state. It was achieved when Arab nationalism was in its infancy and the Ottoman Empire was in its disintegration stage. No Jewish colonization could have been achieved had it been delayed by even 20 years. Not only was the timing critical in achieving the establishment of the state, but also, more importantly, the social, economic, and political disparity between the Jews and the indigent population was crucial. The Jews were of European descent with a 20th-century modern background and mentality, while the Arabs belonged to the medieval era. This disparity allowed the Jews to fight successfully and win their independence. This would have never occurred if the Arab states that fought Israel had been modern states.

The fact that the establishment of Israel resulted from the Jews' being surrounded by a medieval society has yielded its disadvantages as well. One disadvantage is that the conflict has been prolonged beyond the acceptable norm. Compassion and reason do not carry much conviction among medieval regimes, where such qualms are not understood. These facts should not be ignored by Israel's present and future diplomatic actors. These factors were far more effective than any organized Zionist education, international diplomacy, or declared policies in the founding of the Jewish state. However, the Zionist leadership provided the corporate effort needed to bring all these factors into an organized, well-controlled, and manageable enterprise to create a Jewish entity that could function as a modern state and be strong enough to withstand the rising tide of Arab enmity. With massive worldwide Jewish financial support, the leaders of the Zionist movement mentioned here, and many more, not only dedicated their lives to the cause, but more than this, also epitomized Hegel's saying, "Amid the pressure of great events, a general principle gives no help."

The negative side of various well-organized Zionist institutions, which were internationally connected through the various Jewish communities around the world, is the creation of politicians in dominant controlling positions who have their own egos. This phenomenon is not unique to the Jewish enterprise; it has dominated history since the dawn of government. The rulers identified the good of the people with their continuation in power. They know what is right—the ruses and shenanigans that keep them in power. And they know what is wrong—anything that endangers their power.

This phenomenon, of power self-preservation, revealed its ugly head during the Second World War while European Jewry was under the threat of physical extermination. The British government issued its special policy dictum, the White Paper, in 1939, to prevent the Jews from immigrating to Eretz Yisrael and from purchasing land. The officially recognized Zionist leaders decided to act in complicity with the policy to avoid a confrontation with the British authorities on this fundamental issue; their excuse was that this would allow Britain to fight the Nazis in Europe, and the real reason was the retention of their power. This episode was one of the darkest chapters in Zionist leadership. The leaders not only failed to arouse world public opinion against the British White Paper, but also to leaven the conscience of the world at large into helping the besieged Jews by exposing Nazi Germany via intensive public outcry. The official leadership not only did not act, but also opposed any group that insisted on fighting the British during the Second World War, such as the right wing Irgun underground militant faction, by cooperating with the British in arresting them. This failing impacted the behavior of American Jewry and its American leadership, who were also under political pressure from the U.S. administration, specifically the U.S. ambassador to Great Britain, Joseph Kennedy, not to protest under the threat that this would provoke nationwide anti-Semitism. All this was happening while six million Jews were slaughtered.

It was Winston Churchill, while he was outside any government post, who was the strongest opponent of the White Paper. He characterized it as a shameful document—a crime, indeed, against the menaced Jews of Europe. When Churchill assumed the position of prime minister, he did not change the anti-Jewish stand. What a man feels as a human being and what he feels as a politician in power are bound to be different.

Later on, we will again visit this "enterprise" and its functions in the continuation of the preservation of the State of Israel.

Arabs and Islam Versus the Rest of the World

The Arabs' terrorist activities, of which the events of September 11, 2001 are the most spectacular but only a part, awoke the West to look closely into the Islamic world and to ask, why?

If the democratic West is lacking decisive and focused actions to prevent repetition of such activities once and for all, it is not short on supply of rationalization of the events as offered by universities, various foundations, and individual contributors. This is a part of the democratic West, which is short on leadership and long on "intellectual" debate. As time goes on and the events of 9/11/01 recede into history, the analysis of these events becomes deeper and the rationale more and more fully accepted by these analysts—that the terrorists' grievances should be dealt with via political, economic, and diplomatic as well as military means. The facts are very simple: The bombing of the World Trade Center (WTC) in 1993, the bombing of the U.S. installation in Saudi Arabia in 1996, the bombing of the U.S. embassies in Africa in 1998, the bombing of the *U.S.S Cole* in Yemen in 2000, and the bombing of the WTC on 9/11/01 were all, plainly and simply, criminal acts. The United States acted only after 9/11/01, when its own territorial borders were violated. However, none of these acts should have been tolerated, and under no circumstances should they have been addressed through any ideological and

44

political channels. Only police and military means to prevent them from happening again should have been used. However, despite its tough rhetoric, the Bush administration rewarded Al Qaeda almost instantly after 9/11/01 by working with its European allies through the UN resolution to establish a "road map" for a Palestinian state. This reward for a criminal act at Israel's expense reveals two important points: one, that the United States does not understand the Arab world and how to end terrorism, and two, that the United States does not consider Israel its ally.

There is a Talmudic saying, which I'll paraphrase here, "People do not see things the way they really are; they see things the way they themselves are." In other words, our view of the world, of people, and of events is focused through our own personal experiences. We have difficulties visualizing a world whose behavior and logic do not comply with our way of thinking. Secondly, by way of being an enlightened and liberalized society, we tolerate other people's actions and/or arguments and are willing to open a dialogue with them and always assume that for any event there must be symmetry—that is, that no one side is right and the other wrong. We are slow to react decisively, and we do so only when this is clearly required, preventing destruction of our own physical survival. It takes a long time before we get really mad enough to be intolerant of our adversaries.

To understand the Islamic world in general, and the Arab world in particular, the resources I have used are primarily Dr. Bernard Lewis' and David Pryce-Jones' written ideas and my own observations. The motto used, in the final analysis, is related to a story that Bernard Lewis told in one of his interviews. A young British diplomat in the Middle East was very frustrated since he could not make any sense out of his contact with the Arabs. He complained bitterly to his senior colleague that he could not figure out how and what the Arabs thought. The reply he received was it is not important what the Arabs are thinking—just make sure they know what you are thinking.

Immediately after the events of 9/11/01, the U.S. administration refused to call the conflict a religious war, while many commentators refused to see it as a war between Islam and the West and said that the murderers do not represent Islam. President Bush rushed to the Islamic Center in Washington, D.C. to stress this point. At the same time, clerics representing all the religious movements across the United States gathered for prayer meetings in order for all of them to reinforce this point. These activities were intended to repress the fears among many in the West that we are not facing an enemy of close to two billion people, but only a small minority.

Close observation will reveal otherwise. The conflict is clearly an Islamic war, although not against Christianity and Judaism. For many, it is a war of fundamentalism against faiths that are at peace with freedom and modernity. The terrorists did not attack any country in Western Europe. The United States was attacked because it is the superpower that is visible in its mastery of its economic, political, and military powers across the globe. As number one in the world, it is also the number-one target. There is another idea that also encourages the terrorists to attack the number-one country—the idea of Machiavelli that "it is better to be feared than loved." During the 1980s in Lebanon when the terrorists abducted U.S. citizens, the United States did not react swiftly and forcefully, but tried to negotiate through diplomatic channels to release them—that is, attempted to apply its own values and not the enemy's. At the same time, the terrorists kidnapped U.S.S.R. citizens, which immediately resulted in decapitation of Hezbollah clerics, on a daily basis, until the Russians were released unharmed.

Osama bin Laden himself was very clear in his various interviews about the religious underpinnings of his campaign of terror. His discourse is saturated with religious argument and theological language. In one of his videotapes, Bin Laden, a warrior-prophet in the mold of Muhammad himself, refers to the "humiliation and disgrace" that Islam has suffered "for more than eighty years." If we go back 80 years, we come to 1918, when the Ottoman Empire, the last of the Islamic empires, was finally defeated. To Osama bin Laden, the end of the First World War, with the defeat of the Ottoman Empire, was the final humiliation. The Ottoman sultan was considered also the caliph, the symbol of Islamic unity and piety. When the Ottoman Empire vanished and modern Turkey achieved its success by becoming secular, it betrayed Islam according to Osama bin Laden. How can the non-Muslim world pay back the Muslims for this "humiliation and disgrace?"

I would like to quote from Bernard Lewis:

> If bin Laden can persuade the world of Islam to accept his views and his leadership, then a long and bitter struggle lies ahead, and not only for America. Sooner or later, Al Qaeda and related groups will clash with the other neighbors of Islam—Russia, China, India—who may prove less squeamish than the Americans in using their power against Muslims and their sanctities. If bin Laden is correct in his calculations and succeeds in his war, then a dark future awaits the world, especially the part of it that embraces Islam.

The West associates Bin Laden with the Taliban regime in Afghanistan as the most fanatically religious one. Although some Muslim leaders, especially in the United States, for obvious reasons, condemned the terrorists' act, most of the Muslims in the Middle East and elsewhere have not denounced these acts.

Some were conspicuously silent or have indeed celebrated them. Along the lines of those who deny the Holocaust, some in the Arab press accused the Zionist conspiracy of committing these acts.

What is paramount in understanding Islam and its subject is that Islam is the only religion, out of all the others, that plays a major role not only in structuring and guiding its own internal society, but in guiding that society in the international arena on a global scale. The system in place in Europe until the end of the Middle Ages, namely, the rule of the Church, persists even up to now in the case of the Muslim world. Even Turkey, which has painfully attempted to modernize the state since Ata Turk, after the fall of the Ottoman Empire, seems to revert to an Islamic regime. This in effect puts the West, vis-à-vis the terrorists, in direct conflict not with a political entity but with Islam. This religious position cannot be negotiated by diplomatic means and has to be dealt with by force. For as long as Muslim clergy guide them by their religious code, Muslims will never be able to establish a modern polity, and their economic development will be limited. Therefore, despite their numerical superiority, they will never pose a credible threat to the West.

This new confrontation cannot be conducted according to traditional concepts such as the Cold War or any other political or geographical rivalry. This is a new situation, in which the threat of weapons of mass destruction, though more horrible than those of any of history's previous paroxysms, would still be less than that of an all-out war with the U.S.S.R. However, the deterrence that existed and worked well with the U.S.S.R., because of mutual destruction and rational regimes, does not prevail with our new adversaries.

Whenever the question of Islam and violence—specifically terror—is raised, we are repeatedly told that "the vast majority of Muslims in the world are peaceful people" who never engage in terror. This is entirely accurate and entirely irrelevant.

The vast majority of Germans living in the Nazi era were also peaceful—very few ever so much as laid a hand on a Jew. So, too, the vast majority of Russians never killed anyone while 20 to 40 million of their fellow citizens were murdered by the Communist regime under Stalin.

The point is that the threat to civilization emanating from within Islam is no more obviated by the fact that the great majority of Muslims are not violent than the threat emanating from Nazism was obviated by the peaceful behavior of the great majority of Germans or the threat from Soviet Communism was nullified by the nonviolence among the great majority of Russians.

Germany was a threat to civilization because Nazis and their ideology took over German society while the majority of Germans (the "good Germans") either supported Nazi ideals or did nothing. Russia was a threat to civilization because Communists took over the country and the great majority of Russians either supported Papa Stalin or did nothing.

Some Islamic societies are today becoming a threat to civilization because Islamic totalitarians and terrorists are taking over those societies while a majority of Muslims either support their ideals or do nothing.

That is why it is meaningless at best, and dishonest at worst, to deny the threat to civilization coming from various Muslim countries by noting that most Muslims are not violent. Only a handful of Saudis terrorized America on 9/11/01, but a large majority of Saudis support Osama bin Laden. Few Palestinians strap bombs onto their children's bodies, but the majority of them support such evil and none of the others morally condemn it publicly.

At this moment, the dominant strain of Islamic thought is totalitarian, meaning that wherever possible, a government should be Islamic and should govern according to a strict interpretation of the Sharia (Muslim religious law). Furthermore, the Muslims believe that when necessary and when possible, these religious laws should be imposed violently—as in Sudan, Iran, Nigeria, Afghanistan, and elsewhere.

For all these reasons, one's moral assessment of what is taking place in the Muslim world must be independent of the fact that the great majority of Muslims are peaceful people. Their peaceful lifestyle is not influencing the bellicose trends in their religion.

Thus, what is most frightening is not that there are Muslim terrorists, but how little criticism of Islamic terror emanates from normative Islamic groups. While some Muslim groups have condemned individual acts of Islamic terror such as 9/11/01, not one significant Muslim group in the world, including here in free America, has condemned Islamic terror generally. The leaders of Al-Azhar University, the most prestigious institution of Islamic learning, have actually, morally and religiously, come out in support of Islamic suicide terror against Israelis.

So the fact that the majority of those living in the Islamic countries are good people is of no consequence. Unless they do something to condemn and to isolate the Muslim totalitarians and terrorists in their midst, history will judge them as it has all the good Germans during the Holocaust.

The Arab society is a very closed, large, tribal family society. This form provides the Arabs security against outsiders and also economic activities. This loyalty supercedes any other authorities.

The Arab society is a very violent one. Many Arabs attempt to blame their violence on the Arab-Israeli conflict. The facts are more prosaic; Arabs have had many wars among themselves. Syria invaded Lebanon twice and provided encouragement to various factions within Lebanon to fight each other. Morocco and Algeria fought for years. The Polisario movement was supported by Algeria to fight in Morocco. Kuwait and Syria twice sent forces into Jordan. Libya raided Egypt and Tunisia. Egypt fought in Yemen against the Saudis. Iraq fought with Iran for over eight years. Iraq invaded Kuwait. All this in the name of tribal loyalty.

The internal population is not being spared either. Hafez Assad of Syria attacked his own people in Hama so that he could hold on to power. Saudi Arabia's suppression for infractions ranging from petty crimes to social grievances, via public executions, is well known. The PLO's share in the killing of its own people far surpasses the number killed by the Israelis. Any internal coup d'etat was always accompanied by public and private executions. Saddam Hussein's killing of his own people continued unabated for over 30 years. These are only a few examples from the rich panorama of the Arab world's violent daily activities.

What the West takes for granted as regime accountability does not exist in the Arab world. Dictatorial forms of government control the Arab countries. It is either military men or

53

despotic tribal sheiks who become kings. The masses follow their leaders blindly, and therefore any regime change can occur only by a military revolt.

To illustrate this, you have only to look to the Arab-Israeli conflict. In 1967, during the Six-Day War, the Egyptian army suffered a defeat of colossal proportions. The army was slaughtered due to incompetent leadership. Yet at the end of the war, the survivors marched on foot to the Suez Canal and crossed it in a small boat into the arms of their families. Their officers were watching; there was no protest from either the soldiers or their families. When Abdul Nasser announced that the war was a catastrophe, millions of Egyptians wept. There was no protest or demonstration against those who had led them to this unnecessary adventurous disaster. No Western regime would have survived a comparable disaster. Unrest or even a revolution would have followed.

David Pryce-Jones describes in his book, *The Closed Circle,* among many aspects of the Arabs' culture, the phenomena of "shame and honor": "The Arabs use concepts of shame and honor to sanction their conduct." Acquiring honor, pride, dignity, and respect is paramount in the Arab world to avoid shame. Anwar Sadat's visit to Israel was hailed as a breakthrough in the Arab-Israeli relationship. However, this was something he had to do after his attack on Israel in October 1973 in order to regain his honor and reverse the shame of the war of 1967. His early successes in the 1973 war would have ended up in another defeat had it not been for the superpowers' intervention. Henry Kissinger "understood" this and with his cynical realpolitik allowed Israel to bleed before he approved weapons aid to be delivered to Israel.

This irrational and unique behavior is demonstrated by the Arabs' response to the West's rescue missions on their behalf. According to Osama bin Laden, who is being supported by many Muslim clerics, the presence of any infidel troops on Arab soil constitutes insult and shame for the Muslim, even though they are stationed there at the request of the sovereign country's rulers. The hatred of the United States continues unabated even when the United States is engaged in compassionate missions such as those in Lebanon, Bosnia, Kosovo, Somalia, Afghanistan, and the Gulf. The retreat of the United States from Lebanon and Somalia provided the Arabs a victory and restoration of their honor.

This authentic Islam/Arab societal behavior would have been irrelevant to the West and would have been left only for a Ph.D. dissertation subject had it not been for the discovery of oil in these areas. What the Arabs lack in polity to modernize their states, they were blessed with in natural resources, namely oil, that the industrial nations need in order to retain their standard of living. Saudi Arabia, Iraq, and the Gulf states have a relatively small population and enormous revenue from oil. Their medieval tribal society developed a crony economic system with no regard to the population at large. This provides them with the resources to divert the terrorists, who operate as a Mafia, into engaging in activities outside their own territory and thus becoming a global threat.

Furthermore, the combination of a medieval society with an oil income that far surpassed their imagination created diversion of the vast income to allow the despots in these countries to acquire weapons and live lavishly while the masses remained poor. The rulers elected to use the money to acquire honor, pride, dignity, and respect rather than to modernize and improve their people's standard of living. They are not sharing their vast income with their coreligious and coethnic peoples by providing economic aid to Egypt, Jordan, Lebanon, and the Palestinians. Their support is limited only to terrorist groups. The economic aid is left for the United States to provide, without protest from Congress or the White House.

Ultimately, it is really not necessary to fully understand the Arab/Muslim world's motivation, as was said earlier, just as in the advice given to the young British diplomat it is not important what the Arabs are thinking, just to make sure they know what you are thinking. The solution to global terrorism is to cut off the oil revenue from the Muslim world. This will lead to their reverting to their tribal nomadic life, and the only mention of them will be through *National Geographic* programs.

If the sanctions and blockade that were used against Iraq were extended and enforced by the Western coalition to Saudi Arabia, the Gulf states, Iran, and Indonesia, this would force these countries to eradicate the terrorists from their midst without delay, including the madrasas, which are the breeding grounds for the terrorists. It is far easier to suppress terrorism at its source before its operatives are in the West. This simple policy would solve global terrorism once and for all. This solution would require true, bold leadership, since opposition would come from weak Europeans and their allies, the giant oil companies.

Since the industrial world has a voracious appetite for oil, this solution is not practical. Therefore, as a second alternative, the industrial nations have to send a message to tyrannical regimes such as Iran, Iraq, Syria, Yemen, and Saudi Arabia that support of terror networks will lead to their overthrow. The terror networks from Al Qaeda to Hezbollah, from Islamic Jihad to Hamas and the PLO, will be gravely weakened when the tyrannical regimes cease to support them. Then they will become easy prey.

Of the four terror states, the most important is Iran and not Iraq, as the Bush administration has tried to portray. It is Iran that invented modern Islamic terrorism. At the time of the Khomeini revolution of 1979, Iran created, trained, protected, funded, and supported the world's most deadly terrorist group—Hezbollah—and since has been a pillar of support for the others, including Al Qaeda. After all, it was the Iranians who invaded the U.S. embassy in Teheran and held its staff hostage for more than a year. Again, it was the Iranian-supported Hezbollah that killed more Americans than any Muslim country—241 marines in Lebanon. Terrorism is virtually the only success of the Islamic Republic; it has ruined the country and earned the hatred of the overwhelming majority of Iranians. The situation in Iran resembles conditions in the last days of Slobodan Milosevic in Yugoslavia and the Communist leaders of Eastern Europe in the 1980s. Being an Islamic country, Iran can probably rely on its military and paramilitary forces to suppress the uprising for a longer time. The United States could simply provide opposition groups within Iran with funding and technical support to enable them to overturn their regime.

The defeat of Islamic rule in Iran would have served as a catalyst for the Shiites and Kurds in Iraq to revolt against Saddam Hussein, without the need for intervention by the U.S. military. This would have saved the United States the costs in lives and money that have occurred. The United States would only have had to provide the rebellious groups with funding and technical support. Syria will cease to exist as a terror-supporting state without Iranian funding. Once this is accomplished, the royal family of Saudi Arabia can be convinced to stop supporting terrorist groups in their country since they are more concerned with money than with terror.

The focus on a military invasion of Iraq has resulted in American troops being stationed there, as in Afghanistan. At the same time, the Islamic regime in Iran is still in power; thus it is much easier for the terrorists and armed forces of the Syrian, Saudi, and Iranian regimes to find ways to kill U.S. and British soldiers in Iraq and elsewhere.

Peter Cheyney, an English author, said, "The line of least resistance was always the most difficult line in the long run." The fact that the United States sought to invade Iraq militarily, with or without a coalition, not only exposed the American troops to terrorist attacks, but in the long run will not solve the terrorist threat to the free world. The Bush administration, unfortunately, by attacking Iraq, took the line of least resistance.

All the terrorist groups in the Muslim world are interconnected, and they receive covert and overt support from the governments of Muslim countries. The only solution to this problem is for the West, in general, and the Americans, in particular, to fight them with all the means available, that is, economically, diplomatically, politically, and militarily. Only then will the Muslims feel the impact of 9/11/01, and far more profoundly than it was felt in the West. It is ultimately the Muslim world's duty to change their behavior in the global society, and it is not the West's assignment to impose regime change on them.

A lengthy time has been spent in discussion about Islam and the Arab world in general, in order to impress upon the reader the difficulties in dealing with this part of the world. If it is difficult for the superpowers to deal with the Arabs, one can imagine how difficult it must be for a country the size of Israel, which is situated in the midst of this medieval world, to deal with them. Israel faces additional problems that the West does not. The next chapter outlines these problems.

Arab Attitude Toward Israel

The Arab-Israeli dispute is unparalleled in relation to any other conflict in the history of mankind. When one describes, for instance, the French-German dispute or the Cold War, one uses political, economic, and maybe military terminology but never racial language. The history of the world has involved extreme violence in conflicts between nations and ethnic groups, but such violence was always followed, within a short time, by settlements with short or long reprieves of normalcy. This is not the case with the Arab-Israeli dispute. To many Israelis and to many people in the West, the prolonged conflict of close to 60 years since the establishment of the State of Israel, or over 150 years since the start of large Jewish migration to Palestine, is simply a case of human misunderstanding. Many naïve and well-intentioned people are making constant attempts to bring the two sides together to discuss openly their feelings toward each other. We witness the media coverage of summer camps composed of Jewish and Palestinian youth, or Israel's establishment of a Kibbutz whose members are from Israel's Jewish and Arab populations. None of these good-hearted, well-intended humanitarian methods were ever brought into consideration in solving the Cold War or any other political dispute.

So unusual is this conflict that nobody could predict it would last this long. Even David Ben Gurion, Israel's first prime minister, was convinced that after the War of Independence ended in 1949 and the cease-fire agreement was signed, it would turn quickly into a permanent peace agreement. The Arab-Israeli conflict has produced the largest number of Nobel Peace Prize winners, from Ralph Bunche, Begin, Sadat, Rabin, and Arafat to President Jimmy Carter, but we are further away than ever from a real peace. It should be mentioned here that Sadat, to demonstrate to his own people that he had signed the "peace treaty" with Israel only to get the Sinai back, did not appear at the ceremony to receive the prize. Arafat, on the other hand, did appear, since the ceremony was held before the final accord establishing a Palestinian state.

The real reason behind the prolonged conflict is "shame and honor" as discussed by Pryce-Jones. The very fact of the existence of a Jewish state, in an area that was settled by Arabs, is an affront to Arab honor, dignity, and pride. Abdul Nasser and Anwar Sadat of Egypt, as well as Assad of Syria, fought hard militarily to restore their lost territory from the 1967 war despite the fact that a negotiated peace treaty would have yielded the same results, via the United States of course. The Arabs' ultimate satisfaction can be achieved only through the destruction of Israel, preferably by their own militarily force. Nothing less is acceptable. The more they suffer military defeats at the hands of the Israelis, the harder it will be to negotiate a peace treaty with them. Anwar Sadat opened the way to achieving tactical concessions via the White House "peace treaty" to get back what he could not get on the battlefield, but this does not alter the strategic goal, namely, the elimination of the Jewish state. The Arabs' obsession with their defeat at the hands of the Jews stimulates their Middle East oasis fantasy that defeat must be at the hands of the United States and not Israel. As far as the Jews are concerned, the Arabs resorted to the "Big Lie," invented by Joseph Goebbels of Nazi infamy, as their mainstay of hatred and propaganda.

Evidence that the Arabs do not, as of now, intend to live in peace with Israel is abundant. A few examples will be cited here. The dominant ideological trend in much of Islamic society is hate filled. What is said daily about Jews in Middle Eastern mosques rivals what the Nazis said about Jews. These things are said not only in mosques. What is most striking is that the hatred is so unrelenting and virulent and that it is coming from the mainstream of the highest political, cultural, and professional echelon and not from some fringe element. The Arab states in their entirety, which includes Egypt and Jordan (countries that are officially at peace with Israel), have an educational system that teaches children, from the very earliest grades, to mortally hate Israel and the Jews. None of their geographical maps of the Middle East include Israel. During Ramadan, Egyptian television ran a 41-part series based on the anti-Semitic forgery, "The Protocols of the Elders of Zion."

Israel is in a bind from which there is no escape. Should any war start and should the

Israelis lose on the battlefield, they will naturally suffer the military consequences; however, should they win, the international community, with the United States as its leader, will intervene to deny them the fruits of victory. This trap "promotes" a prolonged conflict and does not encourage an end to it. For the Arabs, it is a safe formula to pound Israel with a combination of diplomatic initiatives, terrorist acts, and, periodically, full military assault. While all the surrounding Arab states, with the exception of Syria, received their occupied territories from the wars of 1967 and 1973 despite their battlefield losses, they can afford to claim that Israeli occupation of Palestine prevents them from signing a final and genuine peace treaty.

So skewed is the international community at large and the United States, in particular, toward the Arabs' point of view that Israel is occupying the Palestinian territory of the West Bank and the Gaza Strip. The fact that there was never a Palestinian state and that when the UN resolution of 1947 declared both a Jewish and an Arab state in Palestine, the Arabs immediately rejected it and initiated military hostilities, does not enter into any negotiations. Furthermore, for the Arabs, the occupation started not in 1967 but in 1948. Thus, Zionism is racism; and Hannan Ashrawi, the most articulate spokeswoman of the Palestinian cause, was forthright in erasing this distinction between the post-1967 and pre-1967 occupation in her speech to the

Conference against Racism held in Durban, South Africa, in the summer of 2001:

> I come to you today with a heavy heart, leaving behind a nation in captivity held hostage to an ongoing naqba [catastrophe].
>
> In 1948, we became subject to grave historical injustice manifested in a dual victimization: on the one hand, the injustice of dispossession, dispersion, and exile forcibly enacted on the population. . . . On the other hand, those who remained were subjected to the systematic oppression and brutality of an inhuman occupation that robbed them of all their rights and liberties.

The entire Palestinian leadership follows the same line while simultaneously pretending to negotiate the 1967 borders with Israel via the White House. This is a clear indication that the current negotiations for the establishment of a Palestinian state will not end the Arabs' hostility.

In the Oslo Accords of 1993 there was no mention of the annexation of the West Bank by Jordan in 1949 when the inhabitants received Jordanian citizenship. No mention was made of the occupation of the Gaza Strip by Egypt with its refusal to allow the people either Egyptian citizenship or free movement to Egypt. There was no demand for a Palestinian state in those territories by any Palestinian leadership between 1949 and 1967, only after the reoccupation of Israel. For Hannan Ashrawi to make her speech, after the Oslo agreement in 2001, is a clear indication that the Arabs are not in the mood to negotiate any peace treaty with Israel but instead continue to work toward the eventual eradication of Israel. The Arab states are clearly instrumental in leaving the Palestinians without a home in order to provide a constant reminder to the Jewish guilt for dispossessing the Palestinians, and thus legitimize their support for murderous terror against the Jews.

The Palestinian issue reveals the uniqueness and peculiar behaviors of the Arab society as described in the previous chapter. Arabist solidarity is always voiced in the Arab street whenever any part of the society is attacked physically by military means or criticized in the media. Arabs also will always defend their own actions no matter how vile and horrible they are, even though they are seen by the rest of humanity. This self-centered behavior engulfs not only the entire higher echelon in their own countries but also when they become citizens of Western countries and hold positions in academia. This self-centered, illusionary, paranoid conduct is not the result of the absence of democracy in any of the Arab countries. Europeans and Americans of Arab descent share the same perspective. Only one professor and commentator of Arab descent has an open mind when it comes to Arab conduct. His name is Fuad Ajami, and he dares to violate the taboo and places his articles in Jewish publications.

This phenomenon has several striking aspects. First, why is it not translated into a strong movement to unify all the Arab countries into one nation? Secondly, if any Arab state is attacked by an outside power, or if one Arab country attacks another as in the case of Iraq and Kuwait, none of the Arab countries provide military aid to their brethren; they limit their actions to street demonstrations and vociferous rhetoric. Thirdly, despite their outrageous rhetoric about civilian casualties inflicted by outsiders, such as the United States and Israel, they never provide any humanitarian assistance to their own victims.

One can demonstrate this irrationality by comparing Egypt's two leaders, Nasser and Sadat. Nasser's performance as a leader was dismal by Western standards. He did not improve Egypt's economic lot; his military adventures against Israel in the Sinai and against the Saudis in Yemen brought colossal defeats with tens of thousands of casualties. Nevertheless, at his funeral, millions of Egyptians showed deep emotions toward the man who had brought them only a cultivated pride of Arabism. Sadat, on the other hand, restored Sinai to Egypt; however, his assassination was met with an unemotional reaction and even cheers from the masses, only because he signed a "peace treaty" with Israel.

This irrationality can be extended to the Palestinian issue. Clearly, the Arabs' support for the four or five million Palestinians is strong, far more so than for any other national aspiration on the part of other minorities such as the 30 million Kurds who live in their midst. Therefore, it is clear that their affinity with the Palestinians is so strong that the Palestinians should be able to settle anywhere in the Arab world. When the partition of India created Pakistan in 1947 for the Muslim population, tens of million of refugees were exchanged between the two countries without any repercussions heard afterward. However, the Palestinian refugees from the wars of both 1948 and 1967 are still living in substandard human conditions without any basic humanitarian help from their host countries, which supposedly fought and are still fighting tenaciously for them. It should be clear by now, beyond the shadow of a doubt, that the Palestinian invention is meant for one purpose alone, and that is to destroy Israel.

The irrationality of the Arab nation as a whole is so unusual in international relationships that it manifests itself in the Arabs' persistence in the claim that they are the victims and not the perpetrators of the Arab-Israeli conflict. They simply cannot face the reality that in all their military encounters with Israel they were the initiators and should bear full responsibilities for the outcome.

The negotiations with Syria offer us an opportunity to take a closer look at that paranoid experience, the feeling on the part of Arabs that they are the victims of aggression from without. During peace negotiations with Prime Minister Yitzhak Rabin, the Syrians demanded early warning stations on the Golan Heights so that Israel would not attack them! According to the Arabs' stance toward Israelis and the West at large, they cannot conceive that the only aggression was perpetrated by the Syrians and never by Israel. This paranoid attitude prevails throughout the Arab world, including the Palestinians—the view that we, the Arabs, are being victimized through no fault of our own.

Anything that comes out of the Arab world with its local offshoot, the Palestinians, whether it is rhetoric, street actions, diplomatic maneuvers, or any other form of expression, points in one direction—delegitimize the Jewish state in order to end its existence. The formula of territory for peace can be applied only to its absolute degree—that is, when Israel gives up all its territory and vanishes from the face of the earth. Only then will peace be restored, according to the Arabs' version of the situation. Until the Arabs produce a leadership that recognizes their responsibility in creating the refugee problem as a result of their wars of aggression against the Jewish state, and settles the refugees in their own countries, no meaningful peace negotiations can or should be pursued by Israel.

For Israel, the reality is not optional. It is a must without any deviations. Wishful thinking can be the domain of secure countries that bear no responsibility for their actions resulting from this delusional way of thinking. Given the international community's attitude in support of the Arabs, which encourages their unflinching attitude toward Israel, it should be clear to any objective observer that territorial concessions by Israel, coupled with White House mediation and White House lawn ceremonies with handshakes, will not bring Israel closer to real peace. It is therefore imperative that Israel use all its public relations resources to match its actions to win this war of attrition.

The Mythical Alliance Between the United States and Israel

The failure of American foreign policy in general stems from the lack of a clear, consistent self-interest manifestation. The huge, complex system that has been established to manage the U.S. national security policy does not resemble Max Weber's idealized picture of an orderly, obedient, rational, and responsive instrument of government.

What is clear is that American supremacy—military, economic, and social—is overwhelming and recognized worldwide. A prolonged arms race, unprecedented in scope and frequency, was the rule during the Cold War. Therefore when the Soviet Union collapsed, the American role in the world should have ceased too. Yet its role did not diminish despite the fact that no one universally accepted the three supreme ideas that America supports to push forward, namely, peace, democracy, and free markets. Therefore, with the absence of the Soviet Union as a threat, the United States is inclined to use its military power to engage extensively in regime changing in the Middle East, saving ethnic wars in Europe, and providing food to starving peoples in Africa. Military intervention is not a method well suited to achieve most of these goals.

United States military intervention to achieve these goals will not work because the United

States cannot be poised to strike at a moment's notice. You may remember that the Pentagon machine required more than a month to put just a handful of soldiers into Afghanistan. It required bases in neighboring countries. The Iraq campaign required many more months and cooperation from neighboring allies. The tactic of fighting the "axis of evil" as a protracted war against terrorism is simply not feasible. This outdated strategic system is giving way, too slowly, due to pressure from incursions in the real world. Such a high level of American engagement also cannot be sustained politically or economically. It could drive the country into bankruptcy and isolate it even more in the international community.

Employment of diplomatic steps combined with military threats can accomplish a great deal more than acting solely with military might after the fact. True leadership, which involves an element of faith, demands action in anticipation of events and requires that followers believe the rationale they are given before events manifest themselves in all their seriousness. This Churchillian-type leadership involves understanding the forces and interplay between nations, using diplomacy as the art form of the possible, and finally articulating clear intentions to the public. To this day, America has failed to make clear which, if any, interests it is prepared to defend. All U.S. presidents suffer from a chronic problem of projecting to the world an image of vacillation between engagement and withdrawal. The

United States displays an image of Gulliver strapped down by Lilliputians, despite its successes in the collapse of the Soviet Union, in smashing the Taliban regime in Afghanistan, and in the first Gulf War against Iraq. More than a decade later, the United States has still failed to pressure and challenge countries such as Saudi Arabia, Pakistan, North Korea, and Iran. Instead, it once again exhausted all its resources on Iraq despite the fact that Iraq was already under some semblance of sanctions by the UN.

During the 20th century, the United States became a world power despite poor leadership. The main cause of poor U.S. leadership is the system by which candidates are selected and the fragmentation of the political parties. Each congressional and presidential candidate can launch a campaign by mobilizing his or her own campaign finances without the party's involvement in his or her selection. The system forces the party to support the candidate based on success in the primaries. Subsequently, a candidate is chosen and elected based on his or her ability to mobilize wealthy friends, regardless of the ability to provide either the expertise or the leadership required to fill the office. Because of the need for financial support to run for office, most of the candidates have very strong ties to the big corporations' financial interests. The voting public is left with no real choice of candidates—left only to judge the candidates based on sound bites in advertisements.

Once a first-term president has been elected, he has only two and a half years in office before securing reelection begins to loom. It is the fact that even sooner, midterm congressional elections can have the effect of emasculating presidents' legislative programs. It is the fact that U.S. politics operates on three tiers simultaneously: the national, the state, and the local. Furthermore, cabinet positions are filled with fund-raising supporters, and thus even cabinet officials such as the Secretary of State are derived from corporate America. National security managers are recruited from and return to leading large corporate enterprises. This revolving-door policy of recruiting staff cannot lead to development of a comprehensive peace plan for the Middle East based on a long-term vision. The policy is certain to be based on large corporate interests, where the Arab oil reigns supreme over Israeli sand. In addition, this form of random appointments from a large field of candidates gives rise to an interdepartmental rivalry to the point of a complete absence of coordination among the various departments. Some administrations have appointed a few well-connected academics that do not have the needed real-life experience in either diplomacy or conflict resolution to conduct foreign policy. Retired general Anthony Zinni has commented, "We should believe that a stable world is a better place for us. If you had a policy and a forward-leaning engagement strategy, the United States would make much greater difference to the world. It would intervene earlier and pick fights better." But such strategy is much easier for regular citizens to understand than for elected politicians to understand.

In Europe the parliamentary system dominates political life; therefore the party discipline is highly concentrated, and a special nominating committee elects member candidates based on a long period of firsthand knowledge of and acquaintance with their ability. The higher echelons of each party consist of full-time professional and career politicians who have witnessed and developed their political skills through real-world experiences. Leaders like Winston Churchill could not have been elected under the U.S. system.

In the past, the American leaders failed miserably to act in anticipation of events, which is the hallmark of leadership. It was FDR who allowed Nazi Germany to defeat almost the entire European Continent and to invade the U.S.S.R. before he interfered militarily. He did so only after the Japanese in Pearl Harbor destroyed the U.S. Navy. This belated act cost millions of lives more than if he had acted after the Nazi invasion of Poland. It was FDR, again, who agreed with Stalin's urging in the Teheran Conference (held between November 28 and December 1, 1943) to invade Europe from Normandy, Europe's most western point, rather than continuing the strong offensive drive through Italy at the urging of Winston Churchill. FDR could not foresee Stalin's intention of conquering and subjugating Eastern Europe. Had he listened to Churchill, the Western allies entering through Central Europe would have prevented the Russians from occupying Europe from the east and would have saved Eastern Europe. Harry Truman, too, failed to take full advantage of his sole possession of the atomic bomb at the end of the Second World War to force the U.S.S.R. to pull back from Eastern Europe. Truman failed to force the U.S.S.R. to back off from its 1948 land blockade of West Berlin. The Western allies, instead, resorted to a costly and lengthy airlift to supply West Berlin. Jimmy Carter stood idle and confused while the Iranians stormed the U.S. embassy in Teheran and kept its staff hostage for over a year. He "acted" in a similar fashion when the Soviet Union invaded Afghanistan in 1980; his only reaction was to boycott the Moscow Summer Olympics that year.

When the marine barracks were bombed in 1982 in Lebanon, President Reagan quickly used what is called diplomatically a "strategic redeployment," but in reality was nothing more than putting his tail between his legs, and simply retreated and abandoned Lebanon. To demonstrate "U.S. prowess" he sent the navy to shell, indiscriminately, the coast of Beirut, inflicting casualties on innocent civilians. That's the true beginning of the belief that America will do nothing if you attack it.

The lack of foresight on the part of the U.S. leadership is demonstrated further by the following events: the World Trade Center bombing in 1993, which killed six people; the

1995 bombing that killed five U.S. military personnel in Saudi Arabia; the 1996 Khobar Towers bombing in Saudi Arabia, which killed 19 U.S. servicemen; the 1998 bombing of U.S. embassies in Africa, which killed 224 people; and the 2000 bombing of the *U.S.S. Cole,* which killed 17 U.S. sailors. All these events passed without any major U.S. reaction to the menace of Islamic terrorism. They only produced bellicose rhetoric from President Clinton. Only the destruction of the two towers of the World Trade Center finally provoked President Bush to a military response in Afghanistan and Iraq. However, this action, like the presidential actions of the past, was a bit too little and too late and did not address the source of the Islamic terrorism. The credo that drives Islamism—extremist Salafism—is not just an anti-American rhetoric, but also anti-modern civilization rhetoric. Islamists see all modern civilization as the "font of evil." They may not have tanks and planes, but they do have a substantial support base in the mainstream Islamic world that includes unlimited funds from the Islamic oil-producing countries. Stopping terrorism requires a multilateral coordination to cut off these funds, either by blocking oil sales from these Islamic countries until they flush out any terrorist organizations from their territories or by forcing regime change toward governments that are cooperative with worldwide intelligence and law enforcement organizations. This type of foresighted policy requires strong leadership devoid of any obligations to the corporate world, which is heavily invested in those countries.

Oil and inertia are powerful factors not only in nature but in politics as well. The long tradition in the United States, that business and government should work hand in hand in advancing the "national interest," goes as far back as the FDR administration. FDR met King Saud in February 1945 and promised the king that the United States would replace Great Britain in protecting his kingdom and would not support the establishment of a Jewish state. In the Persian Gulf region, the United States protects these business interests by not attacking the countries that harbor and condone terrorists. Most of the corrupt, feudalistic regimes of the Persian Gulf continue to thrive because they support terrorists in order to prevent the terrorists from attacking them. The United States then is forced to use its own military actions and intelligence agencies to locate the terrorists instead of asking these countries to cooperate and thereby stop terrorism at its source. A clear example of this was during the oil embargo that Saudi Arabia imposed on the United States in 1973 when the Egyptians and the Syrians attacked Israel. While the Americans suffered long lines at the gas station and oil prices rose at an unprecedented pace, President Nixon elected to do nothing. He could have very easily, as a legitimate reprisal, blockaded the Saudi ports and prevented the shipping of any oil at all. However, this would have been contrary to the big oil corporations' self-interest of raising oil prices, and thus President Nixon did the "right" thing.

To further demonstrate how the oil lobby controls U.S. foreign policy, we can cite the two Persian Gulf Wars in 1991 and 2003. Iraq has a population of 22 million people with vast oil revenue to enable it to maintain a large, well-equipped army. When Iraq invaded Kuwait in 1990 and was threatening Saudi Arabia, the United States immediately got itself involved to remove Iraq from Kuwait instead of leaving this dispute to be settled by the other Arab countries. The other Arab countries in the Gulf region exceed the Iraqis in population and oil wealth and surely would have been able to raise an army that would outmatch their opponent. They could have mobilized countries such as Egypt, Iran, and Jordan to eradicate the Iraqis from Kuwait. The first Gulf conflict could have been resolved on a regional level instead of becoming a global crisis that involved the UN.

The reason for direct U.S. military involvement was that the entire Gulf region (this includes Saudi Arabia) is under the U.S. protectorate zone. These feudalistic, autocratic sheikdoms have limited budgets for their armies for fear of being toppled by their own armies. The United States has but one reason for protecting these sheikdoms. The reason is to maintain the stability of the oil flow so that the big oil companies in the United States can share their revenue with the sheiks. This can be done far more easily with feudalistic, autocratic sheikdoms than with an autocratic nationalistic regime. One has to remember that that oil-rich feudalistic, autocratic sheikdoms made people like Henry Kissinger, James Baker, Dick Cheney, and the those in the Bush household multimillionaires. The occupation of Iraq in 2003, although it was instigated by the 9/11 events, was easier after Iraq's defeat in 1991 and the imposition of UN sanctions. Iraq after its defeat in 1991 was far weaker than in 1990. The UN sanctions took their toll on the regime of Saddam Hussein, and he was only mildly a threat to his neighbors. However, again the United States, for the political expediency of showing that it is resolute in fighting terrorism, provided protection for the same feudalistic, autocratic sheikdoms and "allowed" the Saudis to refuse to permit American troops in their territory.

The United States vacillates between engagement and withdrawal in the region, and yet the Israeli leaders who regard the United States as their best ally and friend accept this policy. Unfortunately for Israel, it cannot provide as much U.S. business and diplomatic benefit as the Arab countries can. It is true that the U.S. provides Israel with a $3 billion grant annually, including $1.8 billion for military hardware, which supports the military corporate world as well. This is the largest *single* foreign aid grant awarded by the United States. However, it is dwarfed by the combined aid given to all the Arab states such as Egypt, Jordan, Lebanon, and the PLO. Israel is still at war against all the Arab states despite its

80

"peace" with Egypt and Jordan. Today, Israel's defense budget is 10-fold what it was in 1967 during the Six-Day War, and if Israel is to survive it needs American military hardware. However, the political price that Israel pays for this aid can ultimately bring about its demise.

During the Cold War when the two superpowers competed over their influence in the Arab world, the existence of Israel presented the United States with a constant international irritant in the pursuit of its full pro-Arab policy. On the other hand, the U.S. support of the State of Israel allowed the U.S.S.R. to carve out a sphere of influence in the Arab world and play a major role in the Middle East from 1954 until the disintegration of the Soviet Union in the late 1980s.

United States economic and military support of Israel has been on the increase since June 1967 when France, under General Charles De Gaulle, placed a boycott on arms shipments to Israel after France withdrew from North Africa where the Arabs had supported the rebels against French occupation. It is not clear why the United States provides this economic and military support, since realpolitik dictates abandonment of the support in order to avoid irritating the Arabs. Many political pundits claim that the United States is joined to Israel by ties of affection, by the affinity of two democratic governments, and by the desire to maintain a dependable ally in the Middle East. Since oil has become the universal dissolvent, some claim that oil has given the United States a vital national interest in Israel. For without Israel, the United States would have nothing with which to bargain in the Middle East. With Israel, Arab states have something to gain through U.S. "influence," by achieving territorial concessions and halting any Israeli advances in the event of any war. The notion that Israel has transformed, for the United States, from a sentimental favorite into an indispensable irritant for influencing and controlling the Arabs vis-à-vis the oil not only is preposterous but also is not demonstrable by historical events. Many in the Israeli defense establishment observe that Israel provides the United States with valuable data for weapons performance by testing the weapons in real battle conditions. This means that Israel has to go to war periodically to sacrifice its own people in order to test U.S. weapons. I think this argument is so far-fetched that it does not even warrant a response.

Close scrutiny shows that the United States never considered Israel an essential or nonessential partner in any of its moves in the Middle East. The support Israel is receiving is a combination of successful Jewish and Christian Right lobbying, which takes advantage of the level of fragmentation among the political branches, specifically among the members of Congress. The congressional sympathy toward Israel is still well rooted since it is not being scrutinized by pure realpolitik as in the White House and State Department. The cabinet, especially the State Department, is being scrutinized to a fuller degree. Congress, although a legislative body, micromanages the executive branch throughout the government, from the regulatory agencies to the Pentagon and the State Department. Congress consists of a de facto 535 Secretaries of State, each—through the committee hearing process, press releases, subpoena power, and even direct contact with foreign officials and sometime dissidents—attempting to establish U.S. foreign policy. It is only in this area of congressional representation that Israel, through its Jewish lobby and the Christian Right, can have some clout.

The schizophrenic attitude of the United States toward Israel cannot sustain itself for long and is demonstrably unrealistic. This attitude is similar to that of the U.S. toward Taiwan. Mainland China is worth more than little Taiwan, and therefore the United States provides a defense posture to Taiwan that is based on the days when the United States opposed Communist China. This may or may not be guaranteed once the Mainland Chinese decide to attack. As the People's Republic of China becomes a superpower and its economic ties with the United States become substantial, the U.S. support for Taiwan will cease. Even today, the Taiwanese are fully aware that at a critical point the U.S. will back off from defending them. The Arabs would like to duplicate this with the "Taiwanization of Israel" by using their global dominance as oil suppliers. So far, they have been partially successful. They managed to evict the Israelis from Sinai and created global support for the establishment of a Palestinian state, after the 9/11 terrorist acts, despite a statement from the White House that it would not yield to terrorists.

The European Union (EU) countries, which are similar to the United States in their cultural, polity, and economic structure and global aspirations, support almost unconditionally the 300 million Arabs, with their vast oil reserves, over Israel. The EU also supports the People's Republic of China over Taiwan. One can only conclude that the limited support the United States provides Israel almost defies logic and that its future is in question.

The result of this schizophrenic attitude displayed by the United States is to prevent Israel from gaining both political and strategic territories for its open space as a result of Arab aggression. The United States always applies pressure on Israel by threatening to eliminate military and economic support. Israel managed to retain its boundaries, beyond the UN partition plan of 1947, after the War of Independence, due only to support from the Soviet Union. From then on the Arabs were allowed to conduct a safe war of aggression against Israel, that is, win-win, lose-win. They can never lose any territory to the Israelis. Even if they lose it in a war, the United States will force Israel to retreat. In 1956 when Egypt blockaded Israeli merchant ships from crossing the Suez Canal and launched terrorist groups to penetrate and attack Israeli civilians, Israel conquered Sinai only to be forced to leave. Eisenhower received assurance from Egypt

84

that it would allow Israeli ships to cross through the Suez Canal. However, when Egypt set up another blockade in 1967, President Johnson refused to escort Israeli ships through the canal as Eisenhower had agreed to do in his 1956 memorandum to Israel.

In the 1967 Six-Day War, Israel was "allowed" to keep the territories that it occupied only because the United States was deeply involved in Vietnam and President Johnson wanted to "punish" the Soviet Union for supporting the North Vietnamese by refusing to force the Israelis out of their occupied territories. However, by the time the Nixon administration was in office, the talk in the State Department concentrated on plans for an Israeli withdrawal.

When Nasser initiated the war of attrition at the end of the Six-Day War by bombarding the Israeli forces along 150 kilometers of the Suez Canal, Israel retaliated with commando forays deep into Egypt and air strikes along the canal and deep into Egypt. The Soviets supplied Egypt with the latest anti-aircraft missiles such as SAM 4 and SAM 6 and the latest aircraft that limited Israeli air force maneuverability. This arms race escalated to the deployment of not only Soviet technicians but also Russian active-duty pilots. This escalation by the Soviet Union, which violated the understanding of the Cold War status quo, proceeded without any protest from the United States or with the United States providing its latest arsenal to counterbalance to U.S.S.R.

The Yom Kippur War in 1973 was a complete reversal. The war coincided with U.S. involvement in peace negotiations with the North Vietnamese; and for the first time in its history, Israel was in a desperate situation. Israeli losses in manpower and equipment reached a critical point and seemed to portend a possible defeat. The United States not only did everything in its power, prior to the start of the war, to make sure Israel would not use any preemptive strike, but as a "reward" for Israel's compliance refused to supply the needed hardware despite urgent appeals from the Israelis. This refusal continued despite a massive supply of military hardware (600 tons per day) by the Soviet Union to Egypt and Syria. Only after seven days of deliveries of modern military equipment to Egypt and Syria, which exceeded 2,000 tons, and a direct appeal by Prime Minster Golda Meir to President Nixon, did the first supply of spare parts arrive in Israel. Delivery of aircraft was delayed a few more days. All the while, Henry Kissinger negotiated with Russia a possible cease-fire and a stoppage to weapons delivery. The Russians refused to go along unless Israel agreed to withdraw to its pre-June 1967 borders.

By October 15-17, the tide of the war had started to reverse as Israel crossed the Suez Canal and threatened to encircle the Egyptian Third Army and the Syrians were pushed back behind the cease-fire line. At that point, the "friendly" United States, with Henry Kissinger at the helm, rushed to Moscow (the famous "shuttle diplomacy") to comply with the Soviet Union's request for a cease-fire. It was a puzzle to many commentators why Kissinger went to Moscow instead of the Russians coming to the United States, since it was Russia that had the urgent desire for a cease-fire. The answer is that Kissinger did this in order to deceive the Israelis into believing that they had time to destroy the Egyptian army stationed on the east bank of the Suez Canal. Kissinger pretended that his mission to Moscow was to avert the threat of Russian troops being deployed in the region and not to agree to a cease-fire. During the 1973 Yom Kippur War, the stakes were much lower despite the oil embargo coordinated and orchestrated by the big oil companies. Nevertheless, the Soviet Union threatened to send troops after its allies had attacked America's "ally" by surprise. Instead of insisting that it was unacceptable to introduce armed forces into a place where neither power had used them before and to risk a direct confrontation of the two superpowers that might lead to World War III, the United States insisted that Israel retreat. This reward by the United States to the Russians and their clients, Egypt and Syria, can speak volumes for the United States as an "ally" of Israel and as an "adversary" of the Arabs, according to Arab propaganda. The United States will always crumble to Arab pressures since the Arabs are always united against Israel. Israel is unable to conduct its own policy because of the U.S. threat to cut its foreign aid, and thus it is forced to abide by the United States' "diplomatic initiatives," which only prolong the conflict.

After the Sadat visits to Israel in 1977, President Carter invited the Israeli and Egyptian delegates to Camp David. Moshe Dayan joined Begin for the negotiations with President Sadat of Egypt. Dayan declared, before leaving for the United States, that faced with the choice between having peace and keeping Sharem-Al-Sheik, he preferred the latter. However, after returning from signing the peace accord, he reported that the U.S. pressure was too overwhelming. All of the negotiations with Egypt were handled one-on-one between President Carter and Sadat and between President Carter and Begin. There were no direct negotiations between Egypt and Israel. The U.S. behavior toward Israel during the first Gulf War was even worse. It was what I would call humiliating because the United States refused to provide Israel with the proper assistance in defending itself from the Iraqi missiles. After that Jim Baker came and dragged Prime Minister Shamir to the Madrid Conference.

The U.S. "road map" for the creation of a Palestinian state by Israel, without any Arab nations' sharing responsibility for the new state, shows the bias toward the Arabs. In a piece in the *Washington Post,* Brent Scowcroft called on the new Bush administration to follow its early diplomatic triumph at the UN over Iraq with a new initiative. The new initiative would involve "devoting the same kind of skill, audacity and laser-like attention to the Israeli-Palestinian issue"—an honest attempt to resolve "the one issue that is the primary lens through which the Arab world views the United States." This is really a surprise. The Arabs, who would like to eliminate Israel, set for the superpower United States, after the events of 9/11, the priority of addressing its own critical security problems. To the United States and the Europeans, the 1921 British and French colonial imperial power that arbitrarily created Syria, Lebanon, Jordan, and Iraq while ignoring the Kurds (an old nation with aspirations for their own independent country), was forbidden. To the Western powers, the territorial integrity of Iraq, Syria, Iran, and Turkey is the paramount issue. The Palestinian entity uses a Western name invented only because of the creation of Israel. The Palestinian entity is by far the most important issue to be resolved because, to repeat Scowcroft's words, it is "the one issue that is the primary lens through which the Arab world views the United States."

The pundits, following their fair and even-handed policy, universally accept all this. This is another example of the United States' vacillation between adventurism and appeasement, despite the U.S. president's bellicose rhetoric to the effect that the United States will never yield to terrorists. Perhaps next time, if the Arabs blow up the Capitol, they will request that the United States stop any economic and military support for Israel. After the establishment of the Palestinian state, this economic and political support will be once again "the one issue that is the primary lens through which the Arab world views the United States." After this policy declaration by the United States, if the United States can still be considered an ally of Israel, then we will need a new definition for what constitutes an adversary.

During the Cold War, it was said that Israel was a thorn in the side of the United States since it prevented the Arabists in the State Department from smoothly conducting their realpolitik in the Middle East. Specifically, the disappearance of Israel would ease the U.S. diplomatic maneuvers in the Middle East. At the same time, the Soviet Union was able to continue penetration of its influence over the Arab world due to the existence of Israel. The curious fact is that with the end of the Cold War and the collapse of the Soviet Union, the Arab states have no alternative but to be dependent on the United States for military and economic support. The United States continues to practice its failed policy of bias toward the Arabs. Instead of rising to the occasion and changing its policies, the United States continues to prevent full support for Israel and continues to see Israel as a thorn in its side.

The financial and limited military cooperation of the United States with Israel does not coincide with any political support and thus forces Israel to be weakened and unable to break out of the syndrome of a "garrison state." This U.S. limited support, whether intentionally or unintentionally, de facto guarantees Israel's dependency on the United States and keeps the political institutions in Israel in a stagnant and frozen state so that Israel is unable to fulfill its own self-interest agenda. In summary, this limited economic and weaponry support politically allows the United States to repeatedly strike at Israel's interests with impunity, as shown in the following:

- FDR's decision not to bomb the Nazi death camps and the railroads leading to them, despite the urging of Winston Churchill to do so (at the same time, FDR promised King Saud that the United States would oppose the establishment of a Jewish state)
- The attempt to prevent the establishment of the state in the UN in 1947
- Imposition of a weapons embargo that lasted until 1956
- Constant pressure on Israel for territorial concessions
- Denial of Israel the fruits of its military victories
- Causing difficulties in fighting terror even after 9/11/01
- Weakening of Israel's military industry by constantly preventing exportation of products
- Allowing the Arabs' blacklist, which boycotts Israel, to operate against U.S. companies
- Constant criticism of Israeli policies, helping to delegitimize Israel in the eyes of the world at large, the Jewish leadership abroad, and influential segments of the Israeli society

The most dangerous aspect, for Israel, was the firm belief in Washington that the Arabs wanted to be "like us" and therefore could, and should, be coached into following U.S. policies. When these policies started collapsing, Israel was there to be pressured into saving them. This logic would be at the core of the political adventure called the "peace process" or the "road map for peace."

As for Israel, it lacked international support after it attacked first, in 1967, following Arab provocation. Losing international support, again, after waiting to be attacked in 1973, resulted in even greater setbacks. As a result, Israel's conclusion was not that force alone could not guarantee its safety, but rather that the amount of force it possessed was insufficient. This impels Israel to develop weapons of mass destruction, such as nuclear weapons, to guarantee that it will not lose all its support everywhere. Currently because the United States is the sole superpower, after the collapse of the Soviet Union, the Arab states no longer have the option of appealing to the U.S.S.R. for political and material support and are forced to rely on the United States. At the same time the collapse of the U.S.S.R. allowed the United States to attack Iraq twice in the name of world peace. Therefore, for the United States to allow Israel to be in this situation defies any international logic and proves once again that the United States is not really an ally.

Israel's Geopolitical Predicament

Israel's geopolitical situation is precarious at best. Its existence almost defies any sound political analysis. It is located in an 8,800 square mile area surrounded by 300 million Arabs and 1.5 billion Muslims, all of whom, without exception, do not recognize its existence and view it as an affront to the Muslim world that should be uprooted from the region. Despite some diplomatic maneuvers in recent times, as I indicated earlier, the Arabs' view has not changed one iota in the last 100 years. The Arabs use their diplomatic maneuvers to send a message to the world that it is paramount for only Israel to solve the Palestinian question, which the Palestinians equate with the elimination of Israel, either at once or through stages. This struggle is not, as many in the West would like one to believe, between Israelis and Palestinians, but between Israel and the entire Arab world.

What allowed the creation of Israel, as a well-organized Western European society versus a backward, medieval tribal Arab society, can also bring Israel's demise, since the same backward, medieval tribal Arab society refuses to bring the conflict to a peaceful ending as is done in the West. At the same time Israel's well-organized Western European society is crumbling under the liberal approach suggesting that the Arabs are just like us and that through concession and negotiation they can be convinced to settle the conflict.

Israel has to maintain its military superiority in any engagement with the Arabs. One failure of will and Israel will be exposed to the Arabs as a "pitiful, helpless" target, which will encourage further pressures. Israel so far has won all its wars, in 1948, 1956, 1967, and 1973. However, in 1987 Israel failed to quell the Intifada, and this created a precedent that will haunt Israel for the foreseeable future and may be the deciding blow for the state.

For as long as the Arabs see a hope for the disappearance of Israel, they will not change their policy and attitude. They will do their utmost to fulfill their hope through direct military actions, terrorism, and diplomacy in order to isolate and pressure Israel to make more and more concessions until it will cease to exist. Israel is probably the only country whose very existence is not secured. Israel can collapse as a sovereign state and as a peopled nation via many avenues—militarily, either by direct defeat on the battlefield or through a war of attrition, or demographically, and/or economically.

At the same time, Israel's only "ally," the United States, cannot be trusted to secure its existence and to come to its aid when its military position on the battlefield is in peril. Therefore it should be abundantly clear that the fundamentals for any negotiable peace do not exist. I have provided evidence of the reality that Israel does not have a partner with which to negotiate any peace accord or any guarantor to secure peace. Under these circumstances, Israel's only course to assure its survival is to stand fast, resolute with unflinching deterrence, and ignore "international opinion." As long as Israel does so consistently and informs its friends and adversaries every time it implements actions, the international community will get the clear message that these steps are necessary for Israel's survival. Preemptive strikes, like the destruction of the Iraqi atomic reactor at Osirak in 1981, are necessary, as is striking any troop buildup along Israel's borders or acquisition of any weapons that could be used for Israel's destruction in order to prevent surprise attacks and minimize Israeli casualties. All border incursions and all other terrorist acts cannot be tolerated and must be stopped swiftly, since the economic costs of not doing so are too large for such a small country to bear. Israel needs not only its military might to be in top form, but a superb diplomatic core and intelligence second to none. The underlying reason for this necessary tough stand is not to bring pride to the Jewish world, but simply basic survival. Israel, as noted earlier, is the only country on this earth whose survival is not assured.

There are several key geopolitical elements that any Israeli leadership is bound to consider in a grand strategy:

1. The fact that the Arab-Israeli conflict is a protracted one stems from Israel's weakness in dealing with the Arabs and not from its limited military might. The lack of

Israeli focus in refusing to tolerate any form of hostility from the Arab side is the cause of prolongation of the conflict.

2. There is a misconception, in the stewardship of Israel, that inflicting economic and security pressures on the Palestinians will force them to reverse their determination to eradicate the Jewish state and seek a peaceful solution. Arab society lacks democratic institutions to reflect its desires. Its corrupt leaders get their financial support from corrupt leaders in the Arab states at large.

3. The Arabs can suffer humiliation at the hands of the Israeli military, but they are not concerned with Israeli occupation of their land, since in the first place Israel cannot control large Arab populations and in the second place the international community will force the Israelis to retreat.

4. A peace treaty with Israel is not an important factor for the Arabs' political and economical survival, since Israel's weakness will never allow it to attack them unprovoked and economically Israel is not essential as a trading partner. The Arabs, on the other hand, can initiate military or terrorist actions at a time and to an extent of their own choosing. The status quo is acceptable to the Arabs, but it is unacceptable to Israel's social and economic future. Therefore, the notion that true liberal democratic regimes in the Arab states will bring the desired peace with Israel is a myth.

5. When it comes to Israeli action against the Arabs, the international community will always side with the Arabs. The international community pressure on Israel will always be directly proportional to the length of time any act of hostility drags on. It is paramount on Israel to end any form of open hostility in the shortest time feasible.
6. The notion that the Arab states are concerned about the Palestinian Arabs is a myth. They only pretend to be concerned in their attempt to destroy Israel. If they were truly concerned about the Palestinians they would have solved the refugee problem in their own countries long ago. The Arab states refuse to admit any responsibility for the Arab refugees.
7. Weapons of mass destruction will narrow the qualitative technological gap between the Arabs and the Israelis; thus space and proximity to the Arab population centers are an essential deterrent to deployment of weapons of mass destruction.
8. The Intifada tactic of suicide bombers is a success story for the Arabs to which Israel has not found an answer. The first Intifada yielded the Oslo Accords; the second yielded Israeli withdrawal from Gaza and a portion of the West Bank. The Intifada can be initiated at any time after any signed and implemented agreement. Israel does not have a solution for the Intifada, which means continuous erosion of Israeli control of territories even beyond the Green Line border.

These eight points demonstrate that Israel is continuously in a defensive posture while the Arabs have no motivation to solve the dispute. So far we can conclude that the Arabs are not giving up their dream of eradicating Israel even if it takes a long time. The United States is not going to support and guarantee Israel's existence; and Israel's lack of true sovereignty is demonstrated by its negotiation with the PLO, which is at the behest of the United States and not in Israel's own interest. The Declaration of Principles (DOP) that was concluded on August 20, 1993 and signed by Arafat and Prime Minister Yitzhak Rabin at the White House on September 13, 1993 was based on the principle of Land for Peace and required the PLO to stop terrorist acts and abolish their covenant calling for the destruction of Israel. Israel fulfilled its part by partial withdrawal from Gaza and the West Bank while the PLO did not do its part. Rabin promised the Israeli public that if the PLO did not fulfill its part of the agreement, Israel would retract its part; however, Israel did not do so because of pressure from the United States.

On the basis of the points listed above we can establish a system that would reflect Israel's vital interests in a case of continuous Arab aggression. This is the only road map that, in the long run, will convince the Arabs to finally recognize Israel and establish true peace. The assumption is that Israel is not a superpower, but one that has the capability to destroy Arab armies without being able to establish hegemony over them. Furthermore, Israel cannot force the Arabs to make peace. The only thing Israel can do is repulse them and conquer some of their territories. In doing so, Israel can improve its strategic depth and thus place its borders in closer proximity to the Arab countries' civilian and industrial centers. This will improve Israel's security even if the Arab countries possess weapons of mass destruction. The Six-Day War established this opportunity precisely. The Arab countries refused to sign peace treaties with Israel despite the declared desire by Israel to do so. The borders were considered only cease-fire borders that were fluid and were meant to be more precisely established in future wars or until peace treaties were signed.

Prior to the attack on Israel in 1967, Israel should have initiated a diplomatic offensive to declare the following to the international community:

1. The Arabs' intention is always to destroy Israel as a state, occupy the land where the Jews live, and eliminate the entire Jewish population. In case of any Arab aggression, during the war Israel will uproot all of the Arab population from the occupied territories and move them over the borders to the combatant Arab states.
2. The Arab refugees are the sole responsibility of the nations who perpetrated the war and not Israel. The sufferings of the Palestinian Arabs must weigh heavily upon Arab leaders, not Israel.

3. Israel's taking and annexing territory is a legitimate act, since no Arab state ever recognized Israel's borders; those borders were merely cease-fire borders. The principle of "winner takes all" applies to both sides, not only to the Arab side. There is no need to discuss biblical and historical borders to justify annexation.
4. The settlements in those territories are legitimate since Israeli Jews are allowed to settle anywhere in their own country.
5. The Arab states bear full responsibility for the settlement of all the refugees in their countries and should be partners in settling the Palestinian question in the Israeli territory to include transfer of the population.
6. The Arab states should compensate Israel for expenses accrued as a result of their war of aggression.
7. Any civil unrest, such as the Intifada, will not be tolerated and will be crushed immediately without any regard to civilian casualties.
8. There will be no Palestinian state, since the Arabs forfeited such an entity when they rejected the UN Partition Resolution from November 1947 and invaded the Jewish state in order to demolish it. Furthermore, Egypt and Jordan refused to establish a Palestinian state in the territories they annexed from the original British mandate of Palestine.
9. A peace accord is to be signed for peace, not for territory. If the Arabs refuse to agree and try war again, they will have to think

about the possibility of additional territorial losses to include further uprooting of the Arab population. This will force them to be cautious or to think about other alternatives. The Arabs' formula of win-win, lose-no gain, by going back to the lines-before-the-war position, will no longer be applied. For Israel, a meaningful peace agreement is one that will allow Israel to reduce its defense budget and establish full commercial ties and tourism.

10. Israel will have the right to impose preemptive strikes against its warring neighbors to minimize its own casualties and the economic costs resulting from a surprise attack by the Arabs.

These strategic aims reflect the absolute and ultimate desires and ignore international pressures. However, bold leadership should prepare the country to face these pressures and adhere to its strategic aims. Nationalism is the only successful social movement in the history of mankind. It flourishes, even today, as we have witnessed the breakdown of Yugoslavia, the Soviet Union, and many more, all at a time when its usefulness in advancing human economic progress is waning. Today's trend, in the developed countries, is to unite beyond national borders. However, almost all countries achieved their nationhood by sheer force and not through diplomatic negotiations. Israel is not different, and its leadership has to recognize this and act accordingly.

In the aftermath of the Six-Day War, Israel lost international diplomatic support as it had attacked first, but found itself with a once-in-a-lifetime opportunity due to circumstances in the global arena. After the Six-Day War, the United States was involved in Vietnam, supporting the South Vietnamese, while the U.S.S.R. was the sole provider of both political support and military hardware to the North Vietnamese and their Vietcong allies. President Lyndon Johnson was in no mood to reward the U.S.S.R. by pressuring Israel to withdraw from territories taken from the U.S.S.R.'s client states, that is, Egypt and Syria. A similar situation presented itself in 1949, during and immediately after the War of Independence. The U.S.S.R. was openly the sole supporter of Israel while the U.S. declared neutrality and imposed an arms embargo in the region. Thus, Israel managed to keep its acquired territory beyond the UN partition plan of November 1947. Had Israel's boundaries been those based on the UN partition plan of November 1947, Israel would have been history by now.

Israel did not and does not have a grand strategy for solving the dispute, and when the opportunity presents itself as in 1967 and 1973 it is dumbstruck and unable to function except at the tactical level, namely with military operations. This started with the huge government debacle before, during, and after the Yom Kippur War, which caused a tremendous number of casualties and resulted in territorial concessions. It ended with conceding the rest of Sinai in 1982.

Today, as we watch the unfolding of Intifada II, we ponder what Israel intends to do and what its aim is in the long run. After all, the Intifada has bogged down the Israeli forces so that they are not doing their normal duties, namely training for war. It also has demoralized the troops and left the urban centers devoid of normal daily activities. In short, it is devastating to morale and Israel's economy.

We saw the Israeli solution to Intifada I, which was the "Oslo Accords." This gave Israel an "enormous breakthrough," according to its architects, namely recognition by the PLO as having the right to exist. The Pope's declaration that the Jews are no longer to be blamed for the killing of Christ made me personally feel more comfortable and secure in this world. At this writing I have been waiting to see the next brainstorming ideas that come from Israel with regard to the end of Intifada II. It seems that the Israelis are waiting for the PLO to stop all terror for a two-week cease-fire period, and then they will negotiate. It may be my imagination, but Israel negotiated with Arafat and he refused what was offered to him and thus instigated Intifada II. Did Israel allow Arafat to use the Intifada as a bargaining chip to extract more concessions? Every time Israel makes territorial concessions to the PLO, the PLO will start a new Intifada to extract even more concessions. After all, Israel did not reverse any of the previous agreements with the PLO. Apparently the "peace process" is marching in a parade devoid of route conditions and spectators. Predicting Arafat's possible behavior change should have been left to the psychotherapists and not the politicians.

Israel should have declared the end of the Oslo agreement and reoccupied all the territories that had been given to the Palestinian Authority. The lack of leadership in Israel, the use of restraint and allowing the continuation of the Intifada to force a return to the negotiating table for further concessions, will lead only to Israel's demise. The Intifada can be used at any time, in the future, to include even the Arabs within the Green Line. Furthermore, the prolonged Intifada has devastated Israel's economy, and this has gone largely unnoticed. The world is primarily focused on the devastation to the Palestinian economy. However, that the Intifada is a Palestinian initiative and can be stopped under the Palestinians' initiative is another indication that economic and daily suffering pressures do not affect the Palestinians' polity or their "elected" leadership. Since the leadership's only desire is to destroy Israel, the Palestinians are being used, with their tacit approval, as cannon fodder against Israel. The only financial support provided by the Arab countries is to the active militant terrorist organizations. No wonder their numbers are soaring. This is typical behavior for a feudalistic, autocratic tribal society from a medieval period.

For Israel, on the other hand, as a Westernized society, economic hardship can be critical to its survival. Israel has no natural resources; whatever economic strength it has is based on its brainpower resulting from its people's high educational level. This know-how positions Israel well for the post-industrial world.

Throughout the 1990s, with relative peace in the air, foreign investment created a high-technology boom, and GDP grew at an annual rate of 5%. Israel reached its pinnacle when its GDP per capita surpassed that of Spain, Portugal, and Greece.

Today, thanks to the prolonged Intifada, foreign investment has practically dried up; the high-tech industry has literally buckled, and tourism has dropped by more than 60%. As a result, the GDP growth is negative, and unemployment has increased from 8.5% to 10.6%.

The reality is that the present situation can be traced to the Six-Day War and its aftermath. There was no Israeli foreign policy decision to be seen before, during, or after the Six-Day War. There was a great deal of debate associated with various proposals such as the Alon Plan, but no official Israeli foreign policy, whether explicit or implicit. Even today, almost 40 years since the Six-Day War, nobody knows what Israel's "line in the sand" is.

It may seem that the Israeli behavior stems from the fact that Israel is a Western liberal country. As I indicated earlier, the reality is that compassion and reason do not carry much conviction among Arab medieval, feudal regimes where such qualms are not understood. The Arabs view such measures as Israel's withdrawal from Lebanon and any of the "peace" treaties, including the Oslo Accords, as an indication of fear and irresolute action on the part of an "imperialistic Jewish state" that is about to collapse. This medieval society's behavior is manifested in various examples such as their refusal to absorb the Palestinian refugees into their own states despite the fact that the refugees resulted from their own war of aggression. This is contrary to the behavior of a modern state, such as Germany. After the Second World War, Germany absorbed close to three million German people from the Sudetenland in Czechoslovakia and from Poland without any enduring problems in Europe.

There is a lack of any debate among the Arab states' "intellectuals" as to the approach toward the Jewish state. From its peasants to its "intellectual elite," the Arab world is unanimous in denouncing the existence of a Jewish entity. Intifada II is another demonstration of irrational behavior on the part of this medieval society. First, Arafat with his Intifada prevented Israel from totally capitulating. Had Arafat held on to his zeal and signed a "peace treaty" with Israel at Camp David, he would have had a state with a better launching pad from which to start a wider and more intense Intifada to include even the Israeli Arabs inside the Green Line. Second, despite the enormous suffering inflicted on the Palestinians by the Israelis, there are no forces within the Palestinian society attempting to negotiate an end to this suffering. Parallel to the Arabs' behavior, we see the strange hopes that the Israelis have in relation to the Arabs' hardship, namely, that it will bring a more conciliatory Arab leadership.

Israel, in its leadership disappearing act, decided to make no decision and let the reaction to daily events be the modus operandi. This lack of a grand strategy led quickly to the formula of "land for peace," which was followed by giving Sinai back to Egypt and the de facto creation of a Palestinian state by Israel. This despite the Arab states' refusal to do so themselves from 1949 to 1967.

The Arab states have managed to corner Israel, in the international arena, into a defensive posture. Their aggressive behavior in May 1967 long forgotten, Egypt and Jordan signed a "peace treaty" that is unenforceable and can be easily reversed. Both countries made sure that they got back their territories, which is an irreversible act in today's international diplomatic circles; and to add insult to injury, they walked away from any responsibility for the Palestinian Arab issue and left it for Israel to solve. In one stroke, the Arabs were able to turn the conflict from Israeli-Arab to Israeli-Palestinian. Goliath switched places with David.

According to most pundits today, this conflict is purely an Israeli-Palestinian affair. It is mostly described in emotionally charged terms and is seen in terms of day-to-day events on the ground, such as Israel's occupation of Arab lands, displacement of Arabs from their land while Jews build settlements in the occupied areas, the holiness of Jerusalem to Islam and the Arabs' refusal to give up their holy sites, and so on. The pundits tend to support the Arabs' claims that until all the land that was occupied in 1967 is returned and the refugees from 1948 onward return to their original homes there will be no peace. This sorry state of mind, which serves the Arab point of view, is shared not only by journalists and government officials, who are traditionally pro-Arab, but also by many liberal-minded people both inside and outside Israel.

In the meantime, the unending and intolerable conflict, with daily casualties and lack of clear direction for resolution on the part of Israeli leadership, tears at the social fabric of Israel. It incites groups such as religious versus secular and settlers versus those citizens who are inside the Green Line. It creates the new revisionist historicity, which puts the blame for the conflict with the Arabs solely on the shoulders of the Zionist movement. Many people in Israel crumble under the daily events and still believe that the key to peace is in the hands of the United States and not their own leaders.

Well-meaning writers who are sympathetic to Israel put the blame for the present situation squarely on the ideology, misconceptions, and bad judgment of a misguided Israeli leadership.

108

They neglect to look at the outside causes that brought this leadership to act and form their failed policy. After all, once in power, the right wing and the left wing followed the same route of capitulation toward the U.S. policy. Begin, Shamir, Nethanyahu, and Sharon, once in office, did not perform differently than Peres, Rabin, and Barak.

As far as the Israeli society at large is concerned, the explanation for this behavior is sheer fatigue. Once again the Talmudic saying applies: "We do not see things as they are; we see things as we are." The phenomenon that modern psychologists call "psychological projection" is identical in meaning—we assume that all societies are based on the same principles as ours. Israel, as a secular, democratic, modern society, is a typical liberal society. When faced with an autocratic medieval society, after a long attritional confrontation the liberal society becomes fatigued and feels a strong impulse to redeem itself by betraying its most important principle—its survival. Remorse over its shame becomes deeper than its sense of the importance of its own survival, especially when Israel displays, according to liberal opinion, such military superiority, allowing room for concessions. Jamie Whyte in his book *Crimes Against Logic* deals with "morality fever." His argument can be summed up in one sentence: Appalling human conditions do not make a case correct and right; they are simply not relevant to the case in question. The liberal attitude is not limited to the "Peace Now" movement, but is taking hold among the top leadership as well. However, it should not be the attitude of the leadership, since its function is to lead and not to follow.

Yehoshfat Harkabi in his book *Israel's Fateful Hour* distinguishes, in adversarial parties, between "Grand Design" on the one hand and "policy" on the other hand. The "Grand Design" is ultimate wishful accomplishments such as the elimination of the State of Israel according to the Arabs' view; a practical "policy" that will allow a "cold peace" with Israel is a tactical approach. Harkabi believes that the "cold peace" in due time will become a permanent real peace. This approach fails to see the facts on the ground. First, all the "peace" agreements were based on Israel's giving territories that the Arabs had failed to regain militarily and not a result of their leaders' change of heart. Second, Israel does not pose a threat to the Arabs, and thus a peace treaty with Israel is not essential to the Arabs' survival physically and economically. The status quo perfectly suits them; Israel is constantly under international community pressure to make more and more concessions to establish a Palestinian state regardless of the terrorist activities inside Israel. Therefore, without accountability for their behavior, the Arabs' "Grand Design" is achievable.

The other part of the equation in the survival of Israel is the U.S. support. The U.S. support of Israel is essential. The United States is the sole supplier of military hardware that allows

Israel to maintain its superiority over the Arab states. Whether or not U.S. economic aid is essential for Israel's survival is being debated. However, this support comes at a heavy price. The United States exerts diplomatic pressure on Israel in order to appease the Arabs and thus, inadvertently, prolongs the conflict and prevents its resolution by disallowing a reflection of the facts on the ground. Israel's dependency on the United States is so complete that it never challenges the United States' "diplomatic initiatives." The United States acts not only as a facilitator but also as a mediator in any bilateral negotiations and agreements. The United States always plays an active part in the actual peace process and thus the parties tend to negotiate with the mediator rather than with each other. Given that the United States has no leverage over the Arabs, Israel by default becomes the party for concessions. Had the United States become only a facilitator in bringing the two sides to talk to each other, it would have advanced the peace process toward a finality of the conflict. After all, the issue at stake is the survival or destruction of Israel.

These are only a few examples of Israel's total obedience to the wishes of the United States. So accustomed is the Israeli leadership to the pressures from the United States that either they are waiting for an initiative from the United States or coming up with the Oslo Accords, which is acceptable to the "United States' thinking." The Oslo Accords were "invented," as delusory, wishful thinking, in order to end the Intifada. The first Intifada had lasted for six years, from 1987 to 1993, with no end in sight, when Israel failed to act, even though its own survival was at stake, for fear of what the international community would say. Even Sharon provided only toughness against the second Intifada without any clear solution to the problem. His unwillingness to reverse the Oslo Accords, because of U.S. objections, is a further indication of how fearful Israel is of disobeying the United States.

We can safely say that if Israel exported bananas to the United States, it could be called a banana republic. It is also safe to say that Israel today does not have any defined foreign policy except maintaining its embassies abroad and providing minimal public relations with the media.

The aftermath of the Six-Day War can only be described as omission and utter failure of the entire Israeli polity. A failure of this magnitude would shake the foundation of any respectable democracy. As we all know, the present situation is far from our reference-desired system. It has turned into a chaotic and disastrous situation both diplomatically, in the international arena, and in terms of advancing Israel's long-term security issues. Throughout the years, there was not a single policy statement defining Israel's strategic plans and vision of the final settlements and borders. The only statement uttered was that anything is negotiable for final peace. This was a complete cop-out from harnessing any responsibilities toward the thousands who gave their lives in all those wars. In a strange way, it was intended as a direct invitation to Israel's "ally," the United States, to mediate a Munich-type peace. The present situation is clearly an Israeli leadership failure, a lack of vision and responsibility. Israel failed to take advantage of the victory in the Six-Day War toward its own self-interests.

One can predict that in the very near future, when the "final peace accord" with the Palestinians and the Syrians is signed on the White House lawn, Israel will find that its geopolitical position is in worse shape than before the Six-Day War. This is so simply because Israel will practically return to its 1949 borders with an added Palestinian state that has been its nemesis since day one. This will surely inspire the Arabs within the Green Line to continue the struggle for the elimination of the Jewish state. The threat of Katyusha rockets and mortars that the northern settlements face from southern Lebanon today will extend to the heavily populated central section of Israel. The new Palestinian state will gather all the refugees from the surrounding Arab countries and place them along the Green Line, which will provide additional daily threats. Any repeat Israeli incursion into the new Palestinian state will be faced with three times the number of current Arabs and with objections from a United States that recognizes the Palestinian state.

No concession that Israel has made to the Arabs has improved its situation. To the contrary, every concession Israel made, to Egypt, to Hezbollah, and to Arafat, failed to bring Israel any peace benefit consequences such as economic prosperity, improvement in its security, or the ability to reduce its defense budget. Concessions only increased the Arabs' hatred of Israel, since the Arabs interpret concessions as weakness. The other reason there should be no negotiated "peace" agreement involving exchange of territory for peace is the simple fact that Israel can enforce none of these agreements. The military option is simply not available, since the diplomatic pressure from the international community will not allow it. This de facto makes any territorial concessions irreversible. On the other hand, the Arabs can easily reverse any "paper-signed peace" at their own whim. They have no concern as to how such a move will be received by the rest of the world.

The greatest testimony to the disastrous Israeli political leadership is the simple fact that had Israel pulled back from all the occupied territories immediately at the end of the 1967 war, its geopolitical position would have been much better than it is today. It can be said that never before in history have so many Arabs owed so much to so many Israeli casualties for creating a Palestinian state in their place.

The Reasons for Israel's Failed Polity

The press is unanimous with regard to the Palestinian issue. This includes the Israeli press. Nobody in Israel, with the exception of a small extreme minority, can see any way out of the current situation except the establishment of a Palestinian state, regardless of how violent this entity is toward the Jews. The argument within Israel relates to how to best to live with such a state. Many are convinced that a type of "Berlin Wall" will solve the problems. Others believe that once the Palestinians have a state of their own, they will come to their senses and stop the violence and the two states will live in peace side by side with open borders.

Many Israelis are unwilling to abandon the fantasies of the Oslo peace process, the delusion that there could be, in the near future, a formula that would persuade the Palestinians to give up their death struggle with Israel. This process of contortion brought up a "new" approach called unilateral withdrawals. Sharon's reticence on unilateralism was understandable. He's was wary of provoking a diplomatic crisis with the Bush administration, which remain committed to the road map, and of being seen as undermining Abbas. Sharon, in this process, was unable to convince the world that establishment of a Palestinian state is a risky proposition for Israel.

The rest of the world takes it for granted that the Palestinian issue is in the forefront among all other issues in the Middle East. It has to be dealt with before the war on international terrorism is tackled, before the Syrian occupation of Lebanon is addressed, before the Kurdish national movement is solved, before the black Christians in southern Sudan are liberated, and before the Coptic Christians in Egypt are given full civil rights. The reason the Palestinian issue is in the forefront in the Middle East is twofold. First, all the Arab states want it this way, for obvious reasons, to promote the destruction of Israel, and secondly, it is the only issue that the United States and its allies (not Israel) can solve with relative ease, namely by forcing Israel to do so. The Arab side cannot be easily maneuvered to do so. Resolution will require a patient, foresighted leadership that does not give rise to immediate gratification such as an instant international legacy and perhaps a Nobel Peace Prize.

The fact that the vast majority of the Israeli public agrees with this assessment—that the Palestinian issue is primary in the Middle East—can be attributed to its fatigue as it crumbles under the daily events. The most disturbing aspect is that the rhetoric of the Israeli politicians, who cannot withstand the economic, political, and military pressures exerted by the international community, resorts to an ideological impetus along the lines of a competing vision of Israel society in the future. We could all pretend that there is indeed a choice between the socialism of the left, center-left, and right wing, not only in economic issues but also in relation to the Arabs. This chasm between the rhetoric and reality serves the politicians well but has failed the cause immensely. Unfortunately, the global media, out of its own self-interest, is being encouraged to collude with the politicians in the pretence that for every big problem there is a politician who has a big solution. The constant bombardment of a continuous 24-hour news cycle demands quick solutions to complicated problems, and thus encourages more and more "leaders" who are media savvy but short on real solutions. This leaves the public at large to fend for itself. Such is the process by which the Arabs, due to their tenacity on the one hand and Israel's tardiness on the other, produce the most urgent problem that requires attention, and that is the Palestinian issue. This issue takes precedence over all others in the Middle East despite the fact that there was no Palestinian state while the Arabs occupied this area from 1948 to 1967; then, the issue was simply not urgent to them.

The present murky and gloomy situation of Israel in the international community as it is being portrayed in the global media, whose causes can be traced to a long history of events, is a direct result of Israel's polity decision-making modus operandi. To fully understand how it all came about, we have to go back to the formation of the state.

As mentioned in the first chapter, the creation of Israel was partially due to international support outside of the United States. In order to manage this enterprise the Zionist movement established a number of organizations throughout the Western world. They dealt with diplomatic negotiation internationally, fund-raising for immigration, defense of the settlers and economic support for the settlements, and various defense organizations to repulse the Arabs' attack. The Yishuv established a trade union, the Histadruth, to protect the Jewish workers and established companies to employ these workers. The Zionist movement mobilized thousands of people throughout Europe and North and South America, in addition to the activists in Eretz Yisrael. The entire gamut of these institutions were ideologically motivated and full of commitment. The revival of the Hebrew language can be attributed to their ideological commitment.

The Yishuv settlements in their entirety were divided along ideological lines. The trouble with these ideological divides was that they were adopted, for the most part, from Eastern and Central European sources that were, at the end of the 19th century and the beginning of the 20th century, a hotbed of social and national unrest. Zionism not only meant a Jewish state for the Jews but a specific outline of the type of society that would be created in Eretz Yisrael. It also concerned itself with how to deal with the Arab population. For the most part these ideological divides were irrelevant to the situation on the ground and wasted a lot of energy as the focus was diverted from the main aim: the creation of a Jewish state. However, there is no question that had it not been for these institutions and their leadership, the State of Israel would never have become a reality.

It should be mentioned here that the fact that Zionism was associated heavily with social, human, and national ideology led to its being admired by many in the enlightened world and was the reason it was supported. However, had it not been for the unanimous Arab violent rejection of any participation with the Yishuv, the destruction of the Yishuv might have been the result. Had the Arabs been a willing party to the enterprise, a dual-nationality state would have been established, which at some point would have blocked Jewish immigration and thus would have sealed the fate of a Jewish presence in Eretz Yisrael. The following episode illustrates the dilemma. When the Yishuv established its first trade union consisting of railroad workers, as part of the Histadruth headed by David Ben Gurion, the Arab workers, who were the majority among the railroad workers, elected to join in. Despite Ben Gurion's socialist upbringing, which included belief in the brotherhood of the workers regardless of their national and ethnic origin, he was faced with a dilemma. After all, the Histadruth had been established to support the Jewish workers and to become involved in building the economy for the Yishuv. The Arabs themselves quickly solved the dilemma when they left the trade union after the first Arab revolt that took place in 1921.

After the establishment of the state, Israel inherited all of these extensive institutions and created a highly centralized bureaucracy to maintain them, as well as to coordinate with the various Jewish and other international organizations abroad. The tasks for the Israeli leadership in the early 1950s were daunting—absorbing over half a million Holocaust survivors and as many from North Africa and the Middle East who were immigrating to the state. World Jewry stepped up to their "obligation" and provided the financial support, once again, through direct contributions and through the purchase of Israeli bonds.

The problem with a one-way flow of money to the leadership of a country with a centralized bureaucracy is that it perpetuates the institutions beyond their usefulness. As time goes by, what was once a useful institution becomes a liability. We are all familiar with U.S. foreign aid that was originally intended as a temporary support and turned out to be permanent. For a crony democracy like Israel, these were the ramifications:

1. Need to support each institution without regard to its usefulness
2. A bloated public sector bureaucracy that reached 40% of Israel's workforce
3. A crony and inefficient economy that chokes outside investment
4. Perpetuation of incompetent politicians heading the various institutions and prevention of new blood and ideas from moving into leadership

5. Need to defend the status quo and prevent any overhaul of the system
6. Need to base international decisions on securing the continual flow of these monetary sources and ignoring the future of the state and its national interest

The largest, wealthiest, and most influential Jewish community resides in the United States. Their generous contributions depend on the goodwill of the U.S. government in allowing the transfer of the funds and providing that their contributions be tax deductible. This has "forced" Israel to be a U.S. ally regardless of the U.S. attitude toward it. The support of the Soviet Union for Israel during the late 1940s was quickly ignored and turned down by Ben Gurion in favor of the United States.

Israel is hailed as the only true democracy in the Middle East; however, there are signs of crises in this democracy. The most important requirement for a democratic government is that it hold fair elections. Ideally, elections should be held at predictable intervals, and all adult citizens should have the right to vote.

Voting is fundamental to democracy. It is the main mechanism through which citizens can influence the actions of government. Petitions, public demonstrations, and lobbying are also important. What gives all these other tools weight is the ability of citizens to replace current officials with people who will carry out different policies.

Many political rights linked to democratic government are closely tied to the ability to conduct fair elections. For example, free speech allows candidates to offer alternative platforms for voters to consider. Similarly, transparency (the idea that policies should be made in public) allows voters to link officials to their actions so that they can decide whether to vote for those officials in the future. And so on.

To understand fully why voting is important to democratic government, one must understand why democracy is desirable in the first place. As the late political scientist William Riker observed in his book *Liberalism Against Populism,* democracy can guarantee only two things: (1) that voters dissatisfied with current policies will have an opportunity to propose an alternative at some certain time in the future and (2) that representatives of different political views will have a chance to compete in fair elections. The primary benefit of democracy is to prevent bad policies from getting locked into place and to promote the free flow of information that is essential in order for this process to work. In a democracy, citizens can always organize, mobilize, and bargain—that is, use information—so that, in time, they can replace the status quo with something else. Therefore, the democratic process also makes it possible for a society to draw on a deep, broad reservoir for new ideas.

Israel has failed to live up to these ideals for the following reasons. Its crony economy, which was very prevalent in the earlier stages of statehood but still exists even today, formed entrenched institutions with the ability to convince voters to vote for their breadwinners. Political power means economic benefit, which encourages the politicians to campaign with larger pockets to retain their power. Almost the entire society, in one part or another, belongs to a trade union. All the trade unions are under one powerful federation organization called the Histadruth. Therefore, people are not about to vote for major changes to this structure although it restricts economic development in many cases. Some of the money that is collected abroad via the United Jewish Appeal is divided among the existing parties proportionate to their number of representatives in the Knesseth (Israel's parliament). Thus, the same leadership is perpetuated without being challenged effectively. The military became the only source for new leadership because of its exposure to the public eye due to its activities. This is a double-edged sword. On the one hand, military people do not necessarily fit the political arena; and secondly, the military becomes politicized, since high-ranking officers are juggling for positions in the military that will provide them with a political opening later on. The constant military and political pressures from the outside have caused the public to fear any fresh new ideas that will rock the status quo. As a result of all this, Israel has the oldest leaders who never leave their posts, and the public exercises free speech to elect representatives to fight for a very narrow agenda such as retirement benefits, new immigrant benefits, and religious-rights benefits. Israeli democracy is exercised only with regard to the material benefits of a small section of the population, while the big parties enjoy their status quo with all the associated economic advantages.

This democracy, distorted from the ideal described above, stems from unaccountability for the flow of money to the country and a reluctance, on the part of both the population at large and the leadership in particular, to take risks in changing the present situation unless it is absolutely necessary. Democracy, in general, does not react to long-range problems and generally responds slowly only to crises when a solution has to be found. Israel is no exception; its leadership is concerned only with being reelected and not with offering the public a program that requires large sacrifices and belt tightening to achieve distant goals. Therefore, one can never expect any big ideas to come up as long as financial aid is a one-way street. All the big issues are left for the United States to "solve."

In the aftermath of the War of Independence in 1949, the main support for the state came from Jewry throughout the world. From 1952 through 1964, Israel received a controversial restitution from the Federal Republic of Germany for Nazi Germany's role in the Holocaust. Between 1964 and 1967, the economic situation was at its lowest point, with a deep recession. The dependency on direct U.S. monetary support increased after the

1967 war with direct U.S. government loans and in the 1980s through provision of Israel with a $3 billion annual grant, $1.8 billion of it in military hardware. This ever-increasing dependency on outside sources, in particular from the United States, speaks volumes on the type of polity that operates in Israel, putting it closer and closer to harm's way.

The financial and limited military cooperation of the United States with Israel does not coincide with any political support and thus forces Israel to be weakened and unable to break out of the syndrome of a "garrison state."

Over time, since the establishment of the Jewish state, the monetary support given to Israel has been a multi-edged sword. It transformed the leadership, with its institutions, from dedicated, bold, inventive, innovative, and resourceful to petty minded, self-preservationist, cronyistic, and obedient to the powerful—and such leadership is a stumbling block to any changes. It is a leadership that for its self-preservation prefers to perpetuate this arrangement. The entire society abandoned its past ideals to seek self-indulgence and material accumulation not based on their own economic performance. The United States was allowed to "reward" the Arab states by preventing Israel from solving its dispute with the Arabs, as it should have, based on reflections from the battlefield. The United States prevents Israel from crushing Arab terrorism, which adds to Israel's economic woes and burdens and perpetuates its dependency on outside sources. The United States paralyzed the Israeli "leadership" with regard to initiating a solution to the Arab-Israeli dispute based on Israel's self-interest. All roads to any diplomatic initiatives lead to the White House with Arab veto rights and U.S. compliance with the Arabs. The facts are that it is paramount for Israel's secured future to mitigate its dependency on unreliable sources for support, but the present course points to the constant need for ever-increasing outside economic support with no end in sight. Since the entire population benefits from this economic support, not just the polity, there is no debate within Israel as to the real cost of the dependency and therefore we will not see, any time soon, steps to reform the system. This false sense of security has to be handled from the outside.

What is most disturbing is the decline within the institutions that deal with the protracted external conflict. The strategic response to this threat, to provide security to the society, lacks consistency and focus. This includes not only the military command, but also the intelligence and armament portions of the defense establishment's ability to conduct any war with minimum casualties. The intelligence is vital to fighting terror, since that is a constant threat. Israel lacks a governmental apparatus equivalent to the U.S. National Security Council that tries to form a coherent foreign policy detached from the daily political ramblings.

Until and during the Six-Day War in 1967, the people in charge of the defense establishment, for the most part, had been battle tested in the 1948 and 1956 wars. Their credibility and leadership qualities were unmatched in any other army. David Ben Gurion, although he himself was tainted by political considerations, in large part controlled his generals' ambitions and depoliticized any promotion considerations. The changes in Zahal (Israel defense force), in comparison to its image in the previous wars, are a reflection of the changes in the Israeli society at large. Zahal is not an isolated island. It is a popular army in which all the soldiers and commanders represent the entire spectrum and all the classes of the Israeli society in all its positive and negative aspects. The trouble is that phenomena of unfitness in the Israeli society at large become fatal when spread to the people in charge of state defense. The long period following the Six-Day War was marked by relative peace, an economic boom due to U.S. loans, and outside investment that created the phenomena of defilement. Establishment of a class of nouveau riche that live a luxurious lifestyle created an ever-increasing economic gap between rich and poor. All this was reflected in Zahal as well.

The victory of 1967 was hailed from all corners of the globe. The world press used superlatives such as "the greatest victory ever accomplished in the history of military warfare." Thus, the process that has afflicted any victorious army has befallen Zahal—

defilement. Many officers used their popularity to join the political parties in senior positions, which led to politicization of the military command. Officers were promoted based on their political affiliation rather than on their abilities as demonstrated on the battlefield. All the things that Ben Gurion feared most and worked so hard to prevent became a reality after the 1967 war.

All the senior officers were admired and adulated, and one party victory after another followed. Their pictures were preserved in hundreds of albums throughout the world. They were worshiped as military idols, not only by their subordinates, but also by the nation as a whole. Corruption followed, with high-level officers having large expense accounts and more involvement with public relations for self-promotion than dedication to the assignment at hand. The defense budget became bloated out of control without direction or consideration for other aspects of social, economic, and future needs. This drunken behavior did not reflect the true economic situation in Israel at the time.

Another example of the government's incompetence is the decision that was made as the strategic belief of the target actor was ignored. In the aftermath of the Six-Day War, Egypt initiated what became the war of attrition through heavy artillery bombardment to inflict such pain that Israel would withdraw without escalating the conflict. Israel's response, which confirmed the Egyptian strategy, was to build strong fortifications and use the air force to bomb only the Egyptian gun emplacements. This prolonged the war, with heavy Israeli casualties, instead of hitting hard at the heart of the Egyptian government's military and industrial centers via the air force and commando raids. Had these decisive actions been implemented, they would have shortened the war of attrition and most likely avoided the Yom Kippur War of 1973. Israel simply mortgaged its future, which brought it to a deep-rooted awakening in the Yom Kippur War of 1973.

Another part of the defense establishment that won the respect and adulation of the entire world before 1967 was the various intelligence branches. After 1967, while the economy was thriving, with an unprecedented, accelerating rise in the standard of living and with relative quiet on the borders, on May 31, 1972 the image of Israel as an unbroken military fortress was shattered. On that day, at Lod Airport, three members of the Japanese Red Army removed weapons from their checked luggage and opened fire, indiscriminately, on people everywhere, killing 24 and injuring many more. It was a long time before two of them were killed and the third was captured. Up to this point, the various Palestinian terrorist organizations had concentrated on hijacking commercial airplanes, starting with an El-Al plane in 1968 that was taken to Algeria.

The massacre at Lod Airport was a clear Israeli intelligence failure. It pointed to a fundamental failure in the strategic and tactical thinking within the intelligence establishment. However, because of the politicization of Israel's polity, no investigation was conducted and no changes were made to remedy the situation. The incompetence continued when in September of the same year in Munich, during the Summer Olympic Games, the Palestinian Black September killed 13 Israeli athletes. This was followed by the penetration of the Palestinian Black September into the Israeli embassy in Bangkok in December 1972. To further illustrate how cronyism in political appointments functions, one can look at the the appointment of Aaron Yariv as a special terrorism adviser to Prime Minister Golda Meir in 1973, charged with resolving the intelligence problems. Yariv was the head of military intelligence prior to this appointment and was clearly partially responsible for the earlier debacles. The culmination of Israel's intelligence failures was, of course, the information about Egyptian and Syrian intentions prior to the 1973 Yom Kippur War that was collected under Yariv. This was a disaster of monumental proportions, with many casualties. The 1973 war brought Israel back to earth and signaled the beginning of the dismantling of any of its gains from the 1967 war.

As things stand now, the State of Israel does not have a foreign policy that can be articulated and defined at all. From the very beginning, all governments saw the post of the security minister as the second most important position after that of the prime minister. They relegated the position of foreign minister to a low-level politician in the party hierarchy. The foreign office ceased being a heavyweight contributor, not only to the outside world, but also within its own government. Its function was relegated to managing diplomatic ceremonies, and it failed at attempts to explain policies that were impossible to explain since none existed. As is the case with the military issues, the political line of the foreign policy was meant only to serve the Israeli leadership.

Technically speaking, there is no agency in charge of evaluating policy issues or of searching for any available open avenues through which Israel can act vis-à-vis either friendly or hostile nations around the world. Meetings inside the foreign ministry are reduced to dealing with routine topics and listening to lectures. No issue or topic concerning Israel's foreign policy was ever subjected to a serious analysis. No foreign minister ever pressured the government to form its policy according to Israel's foreign policy needs.

Israel does not have a department similar to the National Security Council in the United States. The National Security Council aims to establish foundations and guidelines for foreign and security policies, in general, and to discuss specific situations, as they come up, that are threatening the security of the country. With the absence of such a department, and without any cohesive or well-established guidelines in foreign policy (1956 was the last year Israel articulated its fundamental policy guidelines), there has been nothing left for Israel's representatives in the various embassies around the world to do but to act on a very narrow field of options, according to their own talent and ambitions.

After 1967, Israel adopted for itself the "American orientation," replacing the "European orientation" after France's De Gaulle imposed his weapons embargo on Israel as a "punishment" for starting the Six-Day War. Therefore, it was necessary to nominate a high-level personality to be the ambassador in Washington, D.C. Itschak Rabin was such a person. He was appointed as Israel's ambassador to the United States right after the 1967 war. Rabin was bright and possessed a rare analytical ability. Thanks in large part to his personal talent, he brought the overall relationship and cooperation between Israel and the United States to their peak. He developed personal relationships with key members in the U.S. Congress and the White House. He acted on behalf of Israel's interests in a way that was unprecedented even among veteran diplomats from great countries who had much more experience than he. For all practical purposes, he turned his position in Washington, D.C. from that of a mere ambassador to that of minister for U.S. affairs in the Israeli government. However, he did not see himself as such, but reported to the Foreign Office according to the directive of his boss, who was Abba Eban. This did not set well with Golda Meir, Israel's prime minister at the time, and she ordered Rabin to report to her directly. As time went on, she did not appreciate his success in gaining headlines for himself and thus replaced him in 1971 with a colorless man of doubtful competence and pandering style, Simcha Denitz, who happened to be her personal secretary.

Rabin insisted that Israel must maintain a good relationship with the American administration and that it had to understand the principles underlying the formation of the American Middle East policy. When he believed that Israel's interests required the mobilization of all its resources and efforts against the U.S. administration, he did not hesitate to confront the situation. He published, from time to time, "pink background leaflets" to explain Israel's position to the public at large and with a direct appeal to the U.S. media. This self-confidence on the part of a bright and original thinker was simply too much for a government of cronyism, and it was never seen again. Currently, the prime minister deals directly with all issues relating to security and foreign affairs based on his or her intuitions alone.

In the summer of 1981, the PLO enjoyed great military success as artillery and rocket fire against northern Israel produced local civilian flight and worry throughout the country. Israel responded by an invasion, in 1982, not only disabling the PLO, but pushing on to Beirut and managing to evict the PLO headquarters to Tunisia as well as convincing the Syrians not to encourage any more forays into Israel's northern border. Israel maintained a strip of land in southern Lebanon as added security. None of these strategic successes were followed through on, and the result was a shambles. The PLO, which had been written off as a factor in the Middle East, was resuscitated with the Oslo agreement in 1993 and brought to the West Bank and Gaza. In 1999 Israel withdrew from southern Lebanon following pressure from Hezbollah. Israel refused to attack the power brokers in Lebanon, namely the Syrian contingency forces there, in order to force them to stop the Hezbollah from attacking its troops.

This sense of make-believe and lack of foresight showed up, for example, when the Middle East peace conference appeared possible in 1991 after the Gulf War. The Israelis thought of asking the United States for a general commitment to be sympathetic to Israel even though Israel did not have any proposals of its own as to how to end the conflict. Their delusion was based on the erroneous premise that without the backdrop of United States-Soviet Union competition, America's natural inclination was to side with Israel just because Moscow was siding with the Arabs. Itschak Shamir, Israel's prime minister at the time, not only failed to see that Moscow's support of the Arabs was already greatly diminished after the start of the Soviet Union's collapse in 1989; but more importantly, he ignored the promises made to the Arab states for their support of the Gulf War coalition. Despite the fact that the whole world knew about these promises, Israel wasted the time period from the Iraqi invasion in August 1990 to the end of the Gulf War around April 1991 and had no strategic planning to counter the inevitable, namely the "peace" conference.

What is demonstrated here is corruption of power at a time of complacency and in the presence of ample financial support to maintain its large public sector bureaucracy. More than this, even catastrophic events such as the 1973 war are not sufficient to force an overhaul of the system as long as people continue to live a relatively decent, prosperous life. The entire enterprise, the State of Israel, is still, by all accounts, a "garrison state" and cannot afford these fiascoes. Outside financial support, specifically that of the United States, is unpredictable; reliance on such support is costly politically and promotes waste and incompetence. Political dominance is a source of material rewards, prestige, and power for members of the ruling elite. When these material rewards are available from outside sources and not easy to track, the ruling elite responds to the demands of various groups to meet their immediate needs, at the expense of future-oriented commitment. The gap between ideals and reality is widened further by the compromises made between parties and movements just to secure political alliances. Financial self-reliance would force the polity to be more accountable to the nation and, by virtue of necessity, always brings out the best and the brightest to a leadership role that will minimize the margin of error.

The continuous international criticism of Israeli military actions against Arab forays and terrorism, which is fully supported by the United States, has rendered the Israeli military very ineffective and indecisive.

After the end of Israel's War of Independence in 1949, Arab infiltration along Israel's long borders with the Arabs was almost a daily occurrence. These incursions started as plunder by civilians but quickly turned into organized terrorist activities with the sole purpose of frightening the Jewish population. The Israeli policy was clearly defined; the country in which an incursion originated bears the responsibility for it. Therefore, Israeli military force will retaliate by destroying military units within those countries. Simply stated, Israel is not in a position to track down the responsible parties and bring them to justice. This responsibility lies with the country in which the terrorists reside. Israel will punish the country from which the terrorists operate. An Israeli retaliatory operation requires some casualties, which is the unavoidable price that has to be paid for security. The key to these operations is that they must be executed immediately without delay; they must be well planned and well led professionally and cause a minimum of civilian casualties.

This policy was successful until the start of civil war in Lebanon in 1958. The civil war deteriorated to a completely chaotic situation with no government in charge except for Syrian military intervention. The PLO, which was headquartered in Beirut, started rocket attacks and infiltration into the Jewish settlements along the Lebanese border. It was clear to the Israeli command that for lack of a Lebanese government, the responsibility, by default, fell on the Syrians. The Syrians had stationed permanent units in Lebanon, in the Bekaa Valley, in clear violation of international laws. At the urging of the U.S. administration, Israel elected to retaliate by bombing the PLO camps instead of attacking the Syrian positions. Furthermore, Israel never attempted to bring Syria's de facto occupation of Lebanon to the UN Security Council's agenda. Even during the Israeli invasion of Lebanon, the Israeli forces did their utmost to avoid direct confrontation with the Syrians. Today, Israel has withdrawn unconditionally from southern Lebanon and Hezbollah is controlling the border area and threatening Israeli settlements. In addition, the Lebanese are diverting their water resources away from the Sea of Galilee, and Hezbollah has been holding three Israeli hostages for many years without any Israeli response.

The Israel of the pre-1967 war would not have tolerated such deterioration in its security area. The never-ending Intifada and its drain on Israel's economy and morale are a direct result of a leadership that seeks to resolve the country's problems by appealing for more outside financial aid rather than viewing its future in terms of its own resources. Instead of finding a quick and decisive solution to the Intifada, which costs Israel dearly, not only financially but in terms of its portrayal in the international community, Israel opted to request more money from the United States. Even before the 2003 general election in Israel, the Sharon government requested a $12 billion package of U.S. aid and loan guarantees ($4 billion in aid and $8 billion in loan guarantees). The official request was made in order to help the country recover from a two-year recession and the 28-month-old Palestinian uprising. If the package is approved (at the time of this writing it was still in the negotiating stages), the price will be a Palestinian state with the same leadership that brought about this uprising. This is a perfect example of an Israeli sellout of its vital security assets and future survival for short-term survival and for the mighty dollar. By all accounts and measures, Israel's security and economic vulnerability is increasing because of its economic dependency on U.S. financial support without U.S. political and diplomatic support. This basic condition is what determines the type of government leaders and the institutions Israel has.

This dependency slowly, slowly becomes a frame and state of mind that abandons the ability to evaluate Israel's uniqueness in the international community and tries to view Israel's situation in comparison to other countries. Today Israel has adopted the U.S. view that any terrorist attack is no more than a sequence of discrete deviant criminal cases, not part of a well-planned, coordinated, and sustained military assault. This approach allows, for instance, the PLO to remain as a partner for negotiating an ultimate peace treaty with the establishment of a Palestinian state while ignoring its ties to terrorist acts. The PLO bears no consequences for its terrorist activities. Israel has to include only democratic, nonemergency measures to stop terrorist attacks, for example:

- Focusing on eliminating and/or arresting cell leaders who actually carried out the terrorist acts, leaving out the entire PLO apparatus such as training, funding, planners, organizers, and the entire command echelon
- Relying on defensive measures such as metal detectors, security guards, roadblocks, erecting a concrete wall to separate Jews from Arabs, and police arrests
- Ignoring the fact that the terrorists are supported by states that are at war with Israel
- Using Israeli civilian courts of justice as a level of proof for indictment of the terrorists

The United States can afford this kind of approach, which brought it the attack of 9/11/01. This act finally awakened the United States and led to the invasion of Afghanistan. Israel cannot sustain this approach; it is too expensive and dangerous to Israel's very existence. Israel must find a quick and decisive solution to the terror along the lines of the U.S. action in the invasion of Afghanistan.

In the 1940s Israel's first prime minister, David Ben Gurion, said, and I paraphrase, "It is not important what the world thinks about the Jews, but what is important is what the Jews do." Israel has come a long way since those words were uttered. Today, Israel has abandoned any plan for direct talks with its Arab neighbors. It maintains a level of daily reactive defensive security for its citizens and leaves a final resolution to be worked out by the United States as a mediator and enforcer. This not only relieves the Israeli government of any decision-making agenda, but more importantly, any resolution that involves the United States is always accompanied by large financial aid—the size of the aid always negotiated vigorously by the Israelis.

Had it not been for the fear of losing its economic and military support from the United States, Israeli democracy would be more responsive to its dire situation. After Israel agreed to relinquish the Sinai to Egypt, the Knesseth (Israel's parliament) voted overwhelmingly to approve the agreement, with minimal debate. The failure of the Oslo agreement did not result in the resignation of its political architects from any public office. They are still all involved and are part of the Israeli political landscape.

During the 1991 Gulf War as Iraq launched Scud missiles into Israel, one of the cabinet ministers told Yitzchak Shamir, the prime minister at the time, "We must have to react because the public expects us to do so."

"The public is confused," Shamir shot back.
"Don't tell me what the public wants, because
the public doesn't know what it wants. The
public will agree with what we decide."

This incident epitomizes and summarizes the
reality under which Israel is operating. Even in
the most dangerous situation, Israel succumbs
to the U.S. pressure while the leadership can
survive in most outrageous disregard of its own
public's wishes. In other words, the political
survival of the leadership has higher priority
even if this means adopting the wishes of the
United States over those of the Israeli public.
For the Israeli leadership the only thing that
matters is a simple short-term cost-benefit
analysis in relation to itself.

All indications point to Israel's resignation to
the fact that it will never be able to become
economically independent. Israel is resorting
more and more to the United States to provide
protection through placement of international
troops along its borders with the Arabs, similar
to the placement in Sinai. If history has any
lesson to teach, it is that this is simply suicide.

What Can Be Done?

Historians like to talk about deterministic historical processes. However, no historian can prove the deterministic approach to any specific historical process. The establishment of the State of Israel was not a deterministic process like any other event in history. The appearance of the Zionist movement was based on diagnosis of the conditions of the Jews in the Diaspora. The original leadership made an assumption that Zionism would possibly be a solution for Eastern European Jewry only. The Zionist movement's diagnosis was realized when the Jews in the Diaspora suffered major dislocation at the end of the 19th century and the first half of the 20th century, which includes the two world wars. The Jews, for the most part, migrated to the United States as long as the gates were open. It was the closure of the U.S. gates that provided the big push to migrate to Eretz Yisrael to establish a significant Yishuv that prevented any anti-Zionist solution in Eretz Yisrael. The fact that Britain replaced the Ottoman Empire and initially provided support for a Jewish Homeland, and the Holocaust followed by U.S.S.R. support for a UN resolution to establish a Jewish state, were not determined events. All this could have been easily reversed and Israel would have been another dream in a long, false, messianic tradition of Jewish history.

The Zionists leaders knew what their aim was. However, to their credit, they elected instead to use a road of trial and deed. They were practical and dedicated people who were determined to effect the redemption of the Jews in the quickest and most expedient way without any consideration as to whether or not the aim fit exactly with their ultimate goal. In their trial and deeds, they exploited every opportunity and political situation to show specific ways to allow free immigration to accomplish the redemption of the Jews in Eretz Yisrael. They considered everything else, such as "Jewish state," "Jewish majority in Eretz Yisrael," "Jewish Homeland," and the specific boundaries of any future state, subsidiary issues. This was the Zionists' potency and their secret moral advantage in their struggle with their enemies. When you choose the road and use moral means to advance your road, your final aim will be achieved. If Zionism had created a pressure policy with specific declared aims, its enemies, within and without, would have overwhelmed the Zionists and they would have failed. The greatest achievement was in dealing with one issue at a time and overcoming pressure and hostility from the outside.

The one issue the Zionist movement did not solve was its relationship to Arab nationalism. The total and absolute hostility and rejection of the Zionist movement by the Arabs prevented the Zionists from compromising the Arabs' aspirations. However, once Israel was established, this rejection turned into a big advantage and benefit. Israel, in its war with the Arabs, gained substantial territories from what was allotted them by the UN Partition Resolution of 1947, while the Arab population fled to the surrounding Arab states. When the cease-fire agreement was signed in 1949, the leadership in Israel was sure that a peace treaty would follow in the very near future. Instead, a protracted hostility prevailed and the Arabs were more radicalized—and to paraphrase Churchill's famous speech after the Second World War, "From the Negev to the Jordan Valley and the Galilee, an Iron Curtain descended upon the Middle East."

Something else happened in Israel. Once the state was established, the Zionist road map of the pre-state period was not replaced by a new road map with new goals and aims. Israel sank into aimless daily life without a compass to direct it under the new reality. The politics dealt with self-serving issues associated with irrelevant ideologically motivated movements that fueled division within the society. The pre-statehood generation that had sacrificed their pianos for shovels now dumped their shovels to go back to the piano. The road map of Zionism was to redeem the Jews in Eretz Yisrael in the post-state era. It should have been replaced with a road map concerning issues such as economic independence and combating Arab hostility. The new road map was not well defined for politicians who felt that the establishment of the State of Israel marked the end of the Jewish struggle for its survival and a guaranteed future. A second assumption, as expressed by Thomas

Friedman of the *New York Times*, was that "the U.S. will never abandon Israel."

These assumptions are based on an almost mystical religious logic. Israel needs to be reminded only of the U.S. attitude toward the Jews during the Holocaust. No nation or people will get help unless they provide important and vital assets to others or show tenacity in provoking the conscience of the world. Israel needs to establish a brain trust that will come up with a grand strategy for its policy makers. This grand strategy should look at the long-term situation and include all areas that affect survival of a nation, such as economics, technology, international relationships, and resources (natural and human). Israel cannot afford the present situation based on passive and reactionary activities in response to events that produce hourly assessments without consideration of their effect on future consequences.

The aftermath of the Six-Day War, in 1967, provides an illustration of how nondisciplined thinking and lack of leadership can lead to a national disaster. The Jewish settlements were always the means by which the borders of the state were defined. A settlement is a fortress and an occupant of territory. Israel's borders, after 1949, were difficult to defend. They were long and winding; and in the narrowest part of the country, 9 miles wide, a larger portion of the population reside. With the newly acquired territories, all parties saw this as an opportunity to improve Israel's strategic placement. The

Sinai has few Arabs; it has oil resources; it is a perfect buffer zone, far away from population centers, and is in close proximity to Cairo. The Golan Heights, again where few Arabs reside, provides a good buffer zone. It contains one of the water sources of the Jordan River and is in close proximity to Damascus, the capital of Syria. The close proximity to the Arab capitals would have provided Israel with an extra deterrent to any Arab assaults on Israel since from these locations the Israelis would have been able to bombard the capitals with cannons.

The West Bank and Gaza Strip posed a problem since during their occupation of the area the Israelis did not force the Arabs to leave, and over a million Arabs remained there. To solve this demographic problem there were two proposals. The first proposal was known as the Alon Plan, so named after its initiator, Aluf Yigal Alon, and the second was titled the "Two Column Plan," proposed by Avraham Wachman, a professor at the Technion in Haifa. These proposals had the common idea of Jewish settlements along the Jordan Valley, where no Arabs live, with the interior of the West Bank remaining in Arab hands. These solutions would have allowed Israel to prevent Arab military invasion into the West Bank and threats to Israel's shore areas. The Gaza Strip would have remained under Arab control.

The Israeli government, despite the fact that the parties constituting the government supported these proposals, never adopted them or even brought them to the agenda in government meetings. The overwhelming support from the entire political spectrum was still optimistic that modifications of these basic proposals, even after 1982 when Israel returned the Sinai to Egypt, would be implemented. Nobody in the streets believed that Israel would not gain any territorial strategic benefits in the aftermath of the 1967 war. The Israeli government never discussed these proposals. Instead, Israel received $27 billion from the United States for Sinai, and Israel is waiting for the same amount for the West Bank and Gaza Strip in order to create a Palestinian state. The settlements in the West Bank and Gaza Strip are there as a bargaining chip to extract money from the United States for their dismantling. Not bad as a commercial business deal when the future of the country is unimportant!

Absent the U.S. financial assistance in aid and loan guarantees, the entire polity of Israel would have taken a different form. Whether a country is governed by democratic means or is led by a dictatorship is not the result of human caprice. It is the result of economic development, of cultural need, and of security requirements. A regime type is not a wishful dream; it has to be the right form to fulfill objective conditions. Israel has to be maintained as a Jewish state with the ability to develop economic prosperity, and its citizens must feel secure in their daily life. This is far more important than the type of regime; otherwise people will vote with their feet and

147

emigrate. If the people suffer an unending economic downturn and fear for their safety in the streets and in their homes, then to solve these problems a more restricted democratic form of government with emergency rules is required. If this is the case, then this is what has to be done. Reducing U.S. financial support will force a focused reduction in government to its appropriate size and form to match its income. If the United States wishes to incorporate Israel as its 51st state, then the present self-serving, multiparty, pork barrel democracy can survive without failing. However, if Israelis want to live in such a pork barrel democracy with the uncertainty and inconsistency of U.S. financial support and without regard to Israel's future security and economic prosperity, then a catastrophe will be the result.

The key to the solution is for Israel to wean itself off the nonproductive U.S. aid. Nobody suggests that this can be done with a one-step approach. It has to be done slowly and consistently as a road map that will minimize dependency to the point that Israel's future is secured and it can control its own destiny. However, in order for the process to start, somebody has to yell out that the king has no clothes on. This must be done through criticism of Israel by a serious and responsible media at large and not through a continuation of the cover-up. Clearly demonstrating the connection between Israel's political and security position and its overwhelming dependence on U.S. financial support should do it. It is imperative for Israel to create a balance sheet that will show the cost and benefit of the U.S. financial support to Israel and its ramifications for the future. If we do not seize this opportunity to change our critical view of the conduct of Israel's entire polity, that is, of those who are in charge of the country, then by the time the truth sinks in it may well be too late to act.

The solution to the Arab-Israeli conflict hinges on two basic premises. First, Israel has to be self-sufficient economically so that it can resist any diplomatic pressures from the United States. This will convince the Arabs that they have to deal with Israel directly and not via the White House. Second, the Arab society must be truly democratic and nonsectarian so that any threat of war by its leaders will be accompanied by resistance from the population at large. Israel has no control over the Arabs' social development; the Arabs have to deal with this themselves. Maybe one day, the Israeli presence in the Middle East—that of a modern democratic country—will serve as a catalyst for reforming Arab society. These conditions, namely Israel's independence from U.S. economic support and true liberal democracy in Arab society, have to occur concurrently. If only one occurs, the prognosis will be bad.

Israel has to put a stop to any Arab tactic against it. The very fact that the Arabs, through trial and error, have came up with terrorist uprisings, which prolong the conflict without an end in sight, will play a role in any future confrontations. This type of activity can replace the Arabs' tactic of a direct and full military offensive. If Israel cannot find a way to stop it in a very short time, Israel will be doomed. Stopping terrorism militarily and imposing diplomatic solutions on the Palestinians that reflect their actions must occur hand in hand. The Arabs must bear responsibility for their actions. Creation of a Palestinian state not only poses a direct threat to Israel, as was indicated earlier, but cannot be sustained economically and will be a constant source of unrest. It amounts to irresponsibility toward the Arab people and is further proof that the Palestinians are only being used to wear out, slowly and silently, the Jewish state and eventually replace it.

Israel, the Media, and the International Jewish Communities

The phrase coined by former Speaker of the U.S. House of Representatives Tip O'Neill, that all politics is local, can be extended to the international arena. All politics is based on human rights violations and how they are played out in the mass media. The peace movement against the war with Iraq is solely concerned with the Iraqi civilian casualties and the overwhelming weaponry superiority of the U.S. military. Similarly, as displayed in the media, the Palestinian uprising—shown with Israeli tanks and helicopters shooting at "innocent" civilians—is sufficient cause to determine right from wrong in the Israeli-Palestinian dispute. The media provides an instant update, 24 hours a day, on visual events as they occur, which influences the "bleeding heart" liberals who are always ready for every "sob story" in order to determine their opinion on any issue. The commentators in the visual and the written media for the most part go along with this display and attitude, and act to further mislead the perception of the public as to the real issues at hand.

The 9/11 episode and what followed demonstrated the psychological inability of the West to comprehend that appeasement involved a profound misjudgment—that terrorists act in a rational manner and that hostility can be resolved through negotiations. With its larger margin of safety compared to Israel's, the United States can afford to appease the terrorists; Israel cannot do so and needs to be very vigilant and uncompromising toward the terrorists.

Public relations personnel proliferate in every stage of the political process. On the staff of every candidate who runs for office are consultants for every aspect of the campaign, including speechwriting. The same applies once the candidate is elected to office. This confusion of images as they are flashed in front of our eyes does not promote a better-informed public but rather subjects all of us to influence and manipulation by the media consultants. I met, during my college years, a professor of psychology who told me that he had worked as a psychologist during the Korean War. At the end of the war, he was assigned the task of interviewing the U.S. prisoners of war as they returned home. The reason for the task was the astonishment of the U.S. authorities as to why there had not been a single U.S. GI attempt to escape from the prison camps whereas there had been numerous escapes by Turkish troops and troops of other nationalities. Also, the U.S. soldiers had been notorious for their escapes from the Nazi and Japanese prison camps. To the psychology professor's surprise, all the ex-POWs reported that neither the Chinese nor the North Koreans applied extreme physical or psychological torture. Whenever their captors encountered a circumstance in which there could be planning for an escape, a well-educated English-speaking Chinese called on the prisoners to discuss the situation. The interviewer was able to convince the GI that conditions in the United States, under the capitalistic exploitative society, were worse than in the Communist egalitarian classless society. The interviewer convinced the GI that he might end up in the United States homeless and starving with nobody to care for him, whereas here he would never be abandoned. This technique never worked with the other nationalities, especially with the Turks, since they were not educated enough to lose their common sense in wanting to reunite with their families.

What is demonstrated here is that the amount of knowledge does not necessarily improve one's ability to make the right decision, unless one is well equipped with the intellectual resources to be able to sort right from wrong and discard any superfluous information. In most cases, the more educated people are, the easier it is to manipulate their decision-making faculties.

The media consultants are proficient in Orwell's "newspeak" in the characterization of international affairs so as to suggest that defeat is victory, loss is gain, and submission is supremacy. Dictating major concessions to an ally is called a diplomatic triumph. To demonstrate how this plays out in our daily lives, I will provide a fictitious circumstance cited from the book *The Great Détente Disaster* by Edward Friedland, Paul Seabury, and Aaron Wildavsky.

Suppose a man puts a gun in

your back and cries 'Your money or your life!' and, being a prudent person, you give up your money. You lose money but keep your integrity. If you then turned to the robber and said that this encounter had brought you closer together, that this new wealth would, by reducing his sense of inferiority, increase communication and that anyway, it was good for your children to learn to live without money, then one of you is sick; and it is not the thief.

Clearly, Israel is the victim in this illustration and the Arabs are the robbers.

The Arab world exploits media techniques to their full potential in order to manipulate the West and attack Israel, while they themselves are not exposed to the Western "bleeding heart" mentality in their own society. Therefore, their terrorist and anti-Western campaign goes on unabated. This tenacity is aimed at the "soft," "bleeding heart" liberals in Western society who are eager to assume guilt and cure all the Arab ills. The West ignores the agenda the Arabs are manifesting to their own people, which is far different from the one advertised in the West. Their enormous oil revenues are misused, channeled to secure dictatorships of the worst variety. These dictators end up acquiring weapons of mass destruction, paying off terrorists, and never directing the money to benefit the poor or toward any other humanitarian need.

As the Arab-Israeli conflict became a Palestinian-Israeli conflict, many Israeli supporters became acrimonious critics of Israel and failed to see how appeasement of the PLO would lead to the end of the conflict. Richard Ben Cramer wrote the book, titled *How Israel Lost,* that epitomizes this approach. He posed four questions:

I. Why do we care about Israel?
II. Why don't the Palestinians have a state?
III. What is a Jewish state?
IV. Why is there no peace?

What followed, as answers to these questions, was a mixture of spiritual and moral history on the establishment of the state and its right to exist. This high-morality approach applies only to Israel and not to any other country. It is time to reply to these questions as follows:

Why do we care about Israel? Because the people in Israel want to live there, about five million Jews.

Why don't the Palestinians have a state? Because they rejected the partition plan offered them in November 1947.

What is a Jewish state? Whatever its citizen want to define it as.

Why is there no peace? Because the Arabs refuse to have peace; no amount of concession by Israel will bring peace. The Arabs have to sign a peace with Israel based on the status quo and not reversal of past events.

To avert and circumvent defeat in the media propaganda war, the Israeli leadership has to reclaim the offensive posture with clear and genuine messages that are focused on the real issues as outlined above. All this has to be followed with a consistently implemented policy that will convince the other side that their public relations campaign in the media is futile. For as long as Israel allows itself to insist that it is ultimately committed to creating a Palestinian state along the lines of the "road map," as presented to them by the United States, the European Union, Russia, and the UN without any consequences for Palestinian behavior, any military responses they make will be criticized.

Tackling the war on terrorism demands a greater resolution than being bogged down in the war with Iraq and will be a necessity for many generations. While unable to retreat from Afghanistan and Iraq and establish a democracy in those countries, the United States is on a new-initiative path of promoting democracy throughout the greater Middle East and beyond. This ploy is more of a public relations and U.S. election initiative than it is about practical progress. It can only lead to the easier path of "solving" the conflict between

Israel and the Palestinians, since Israel does not present any objection to being pressured. To survive any assault, it is imperative that Israel insist on removing the Palestinian issue from any dealings the West has with the Arabs and the entire Muslim world and present a clear, one-sided initiative for resolving the conflict with the Arabs in its own controlled territory.

The failure of Israel in the media war has caused an outburst of violence and destructive anti-Semitic acts in Europe and North Africa. This outburst, ironically following the events of 9/11, encompassed the traditional African-American anti-Semites who provided proof once again of the weaknesses and isolation of Israel and the Jews in the world. Anti-Semites throughout history attacked the Jews only because they were the most vulnerable of groups and unable to protect themselves. However, attacking helpless people does not fit with the anti-Semites' "chivalrous" behavior, and therefore it is necessary to invent the all-powerful Jewish conspiracy that dominates the world.

Today's anti-Semites have various forms and justifications. There is no need to dwell on the Muslim anti-Semites and their populations in Europe and the United States that are the primary cause for the recent exceptional physical destruction. There are still the traditional irrational Christian and Right wing elements. Noam Chomsky symbolizes the third group, the so called Left wing anti-Israeli element that is based again on irrational and emotional motives. For them, moral righteousness is directly proportional to economic disadvantage, military inferiority, and darkness of the skin. They get confused about the conflict between India and Pakistan over Kashmir and thus their opinion is not heard on this issue. This element supports the Palestinians on the same rationale it employed to support the Taliban against the United States in Afghanistan. To them, Israel represents "Little America" and they simply deny Israel's right to exist. Therefore, it is immaterial what Israel does or does not do; it will always be wrong.

Unfortunately this group has a large following, especially among the members of academia who are sympathetic with the left- wing anti-Semitic philosophy even though they are not denying Israel's right to exist. The left wing and liberal faction in the press and academia's anti-Israeli campaign can be considered racist and anti-Semitic. They use the same tactics as the old anti-Semites, such as conspiracy theory. They totally and purposely ignore the Arab side's "contribution" to the violence. They exploit the Israeli weakness and sensitivity to international criticism of its actions. Last but not least, they are not honest in applying the same criteria to other more powerful conflicts that are insensitive to their criticism—Chechnya versus Russia, Turkey versus the Kurds, and so on.

There is another group in the media who are naïve when it comes to the Arab-Israeli conflict.

Thomas L. Friedman, who writes the prestigious foreign affairs column for the *New York Times,* represents this group. He receives total support from the paper's publisher, which enables him to travel extensively. Using his good fortune, he has met the king of Jordan and the monarch of Saudi Arabia among many other officials throughout the world. What he fails to see is that the Arabs learned a very important lesson from the 1967 war. When their leaders threatened to throw the Jews into the sea, this horrified the West and thus precluded them from having any negotiations regarding a settlement with Israel. With the urging of the public relations people on Madison Avenue, they replaced the threat to throw the Jews into the sea with the plight of the Palestinians after the Balfour Declaration.

This turned things around dramatically for the Arabs without their changing their ultimate goal of throwing the Jews into the sea. They won the sympathy of the enlightened West. That is what Friedman hears from the king of Jordan and the monarch of Saudi Arabia. They urge him to argue that Israel should limit its military response to terrorism, withdraw from "occupied" territory, close down its settlements in the "occupied" territory, and negotiate, negotiate, negotiate. He does so, despite a clear demonstration that the "enlightened" monarchs provide the Palestinians financial support only to perpetuate terrorism against Israel. They have never provided a cent, from their huge oil revenue, for any humanitarian help to the Palestinians. Strangely, with the next stroke of the pen, Friedman supports the war against Iraq as part of the Bush administration's "war against terror" despite the fact that Iraq never threatened the United States directly. It escapes him that the focus is on Saddam's Iraq only because this would be a conventional war that one has a reasonable chance of winning. It is very frustrating for a giant to be bitten by mosquitoes that he cannot catch. So the giant ends up threatening the bully down the street whom the giant blames for breeding the mosquitoes.

Friedman's position on dealing with the Palestinian issue is not the result of deep analysis. It follows from the fact that Israel never outlined its ideas, unlike President Bush in his war preparations against Iraq, on what it sees as an acceptable solution to the problem, particularly in view of the Palestinian uprising and terror. Given the leadership vacuum in Israel, Friedman has concluded that for the Palestinians to negotiate a settlement would be far superior to their vanquishing their terror masters. Unfortunately, many in the media at large, including in Israel, share this attitude and thus Israel is portrayed as the villain in the conflict. The mere fact that Israel does not submit to the media its own vision of the solution to the conflict is a major contributor to the portrayal. I am not endorsing any anti-Israeli or anti-Semitic platform of any color or shape; however, the fact that Israel uses oppressive force against the Palestinians to quell terror while at the same time claiming to work toward establishing a Palestinian state confuses many well-intentioned commentators into condemning Israel's "atrocities" against the Palestinians.

I was struck by the reaction to the Palestinian issue from many of Israel's longtime security policy pundits. They are all seasoned veterans of Israel's past wars and have held very important and key positions within the Israeli security establishment. They all arrived at the conclusion that it is mandatory for Israel to negotiate a final settlement with the Palestinians. According to them there is simply no other way of solving the Arab-Israeli conflict. In short, they all agree with Friedman. It is clear that the Arabs have never given up their dream of obliterating the Jewish state and that any negotiations will involve the United States as a pro-Arab mediator. This will result in strategic territorial concessions. It is beyond me how this can be the final solution! These pundits have never provided an explanation as to how any agreement can be sustained and enforced in the event of violations from the Arab side. Furthermore, if the Arabs succeed in getting from Israel strategic territorial concessions, what incentive do they have for keeping an agreement instead of keeping the pressure on? Why should they not be encouraged to keep up and even intensify their terror against Israel? To me this enigmatic position on the part of the Israeli pundits stems from an attitude of utter fatigue and delusionary fantasia that can only result from a protracted conflict. They see no end in sight and are unable to envision the possibility of any political

161

caucus within Israel that will be able to advance Israel's own self-interest. They are simply resigned to leaving matters in U.S. hands. Like many others, including Friedman, they live with the illusion that the United States will never abandon Israel.

Israel's Shimon Peres showed how a classic capitulation is done while promoting his own legacy for the ages and becoming the darling of the American media. For many years Peres was a staunch supporter of a policy that would allow Israel to retain the territories acquired during the 1967 war for strategic improvements. He was a strong opponent of the establishment of a Palestinian state in the West Bank and Gaza and promoted settlements in the new territories. He did all this through his prolific writing ability in Hebrew. Then came 1987, the first Arab uprising, which is referred to as the First Intifada. When the Israeli leadership, under Prime Minster Yitzchak Shamir and Defense Minister Yitzchak Rabin, were unable or unwilling to take the risk of putting a stop to the uprising, Peres changed his approach. When he was appointed foreign minister under Rabin between 1992 and 1994, he published a book in English and Hebrew titled *The New Middle East.* With one stroke of the pen, he transformed the Middle East from a collection of feudalistic, autocratic, dictatorial regimes of the worst kind, fanatic in their hostility to Israel, to a Westernized peace-loving society with a genuine concern for the well-being of their own people. This make-believe, "Alice in

Wonderland" transformation of the Arab world while the uprising in Israel was at its full intensity "allowed" him to proceed with the signing of the Oslo Accords. This act improved his image in the mass media and his legacy and enabled Rabin to share a Nobel Peace Prize with Arafat. This is a case of Orwellian language winning in the media but bringing disastrous results. Now we see Intifada II, which resulted without any political and media stardom consequences for its initiators. Today, true leadership is almost nonexistent, and the public relations media has replaced them and runs amok undisturbed.

Regardless of the reasons people in the media display a negative image of Israel, what is of most importance for Israel, at this juncture, is that it is losing its war for public opinion. Not only does the world at large form a negative opinion of Israel, but support within the world's Jewish communities shows signs of deep erosion. This will add to Israel's isolation among the official governments of the world. Losing support from the world's Jewish communities can be devastating, since it can lead to the elimination of U.S. economic and military support. This is one more reason why Israel cannot afford a prolonged confrontation with the Palestinian terrorist uprising. It is also imperative for Israel to show its own initiative in solving its own security problems.

The Reason for Israel's Participation in the "Peace Process"

Israel is a small nation whose very existence may be put in question at any moment; a small nation can disappear, and it knows it. Israel is not just a small country. Its neighbors publicly declare its very existence is an affront to law, morality and religion and make its extinction an explicit national goal.

This situation existed from Haj Amin Husseini, the Mufti of Jerusalem, who cooperated with Nazi Germany prior and during WWII to Yassir Arafat, from 1964, up to today with Mahmoud Abbas, the current PLO leader.
So intense is their request to obliterate Israel that despite their defeat in many wars, their campaign has evolved into terrorism, international BDS (Boycott, Divestment and Sanctions) and the diplomatic steps of November 10, 1975, the passage of UN general assembly resolution 3379, which equated Zionism with racism.

The Palestinian Authority (PA) that was established in 1994, after the Oslo Agreement, denied Jewish history and the Jewish connection to the land of Israel. Palestinian academics openly admitted that the goal of rewriting history is to deny all Jewish political rights to Israel.

The Arabs are constantly intimidating Israel for its part in the Six Day War when Israel conquered the Temple Mount and raised the Israeli flag over the Mosque of Omar. Moshe Dayan told the commander to remove the flag immediately. Even today, the Jews are not allowed to pray on the Temple Mount and have seceded the right to worship there to the Waaf (Islamic Jordanian authority).

In 1979, Israel signed a formal peace treaty with Egypt. In 1994, it signed a peace treaty with Jordan. But, even so, the people of Egypt and Jordan never made peace with Israel.

The Middle East Media Research Institute (MEMRI) has reported that journalist Firnas Hafzi wrote an anti-semitic article in the Egyptian monthly Al Kibar titled "the Jewish Bloodsuckers of Passover" that promoted the blood libel accusation, according to which Jews murder non-Jews in order to use their blood to make matza for the Passover Seder. Hafzi wrote: "The Jews combined the preparation of matzos and the offering up of sacrifices with their enmity towards non-Jews, especially Christians, and mixed the blood of one of their victims into the matza dough. This was done especially on Passover, Purim and circumcision rituals. They also used blood in acts of sorcery and witchcraft."

Any Egyptian who intends to visit Israel has to register with the Interior Ministry and he is included on the Black List.

The goal of destroying Israel unifies Fatah with Hamas and it unifies them both with Iran, the Muslim Brotherhood, and Saudi Arabia.
Finally, Israel's withdrawal from Gaza, Southern Lebanon and Sinai didn't bring Israel peace, but rockets deployed on their citizens.

To any individual, it is clear that, there is no desire from the Arab side to have peace with Israel. The Palestinians had opportunities to get their independence in 1920, 1936, 1947, 1949 until 1967, 1994, 1999, 2005 and 2008 and they rejected all of those opportunities simply because they will not accept any part of the historical land of Israel to be awarded the Jews.
It is abundantly clear that the policy of land for peace does not work. Only social changes in the Arab society of accepting the Jewish State, as part of the Middle East, will bring a real Peace to the region. This is the misconception of the USA foreign policy and people like Tom Friedman have no apprehension.

American foreign policy is more a sitcom than common sense. That, in a way, is the good news. Our failures are comic while those of other nations are tragic. Americans do not understand the tragic impulses of other peoples because they are exceptional. The Europeans failed as nationalists and are failing as post-nationalists.

Because Americans are not an ethnicity, but a union of immigrants committed to a concept, our nationalism discloses a universal impulse. We blunder when we forget how exceptional we are, and ignore the tragic impulses that impinge on other peoples.

Only once, in the past century, have we read the world right. We got it wrong when Woodrow Wilson proposed a utopian postwar vision in 1919, when the isolationists tried to stay out of the European conflict in the late 1930s, when Roosevelt and Truman let Stalin absorb Eastern Europe, when we overextended and then turned tail in Vietnam and when we undertook to turn Iraq and Afghanistan into Western-style democracies. Ronald Reagan got it right when he decided that it was time to roll back communism – but he also understood that we would have to live with Russia as a nation.

We have stumbled into the world's troubles like incongruous clowns in a tragedy: we observe the anguished faces of the other characters and conclude that everyone else on stage is insane. That is how Americans view Russian President Vladimir Putin. As Time magazine reported: An Obama administration official leaked to the New York Times on Sunday the fact that German Chancellor Angela Merkel told President Obama she wasn't sure if Putin was in touch with reality. "In another world," Merkel reportedly said, according to the leak. Then, in a conference call with reporters, later in the day, three administration officials took turns firing rhetorical shots: "Being inside Putin's head is not someplace anyone wants to be."

I doubt that Merkel ever said it, but that's a different question. Russia, as Colonel Ralph Peters (retired) told Sean Hannity last week, "believes in Russia". To the Obamoids, belief in one's country is prima facie evidence of mental defect. Hillary Clinton, Senator John McCain and Senator Marco Rubio, meanwhile, compare Putin to Hitler, an example of what the late Leo Strauss derided as "reduction ad Hitlerium".

Contrast that to President Obama's characterization of Iran in his interview with Bloomberg's Jeffrey Goldberg: "If you look at Iranian behavior, they are strategic, and they're not impulsive. They have a worldview, and they see their interests, and they respond to costs and benefits." That's been the longstanding view of this administration.

Just how does one define rationality in global politics? Here is a question that helps: What is the rational self-interest of a nation that will cease to exist within the horizon of present-day expectations? We look, uncomprehendingly, on the petty wars of perished peoples and marvel at the sheer vanity of their forgotten battles. How do we know that someone in the future won't look back at us the same way? There have been Great Extinctions of the Peoples before in world history, but never with the breadth and speed of the demographic declines in our own era. That should give us something of an objective gauge with which to judge the rationality of actors.

Iran's unprecedented fertility decline has accelerated - from about 7 children per female in 1979 to only 1.6 last years, according to a UN estimate. Russia, meanwhile, is struggling to emerge from what seemed like a demographic death-sentence only a few years ago. Ukraine is Europe's poster-boy for demographic death.

Iran is dying a slow and dreadful death: by mid-century more than a third of its people will be over 60, and by the end of the century, half its people will be over 60, imposing an impossible burden on a poor country. Its rulers are taking urgent steps to reverse the fertility decline, opening clinics to treat infertility, which reportedly affects one-fifth of all Iranian couples, against a world average of around 8%. Why infertility is so widespread in Iran is unclear; it might be due to the fact that the reported incidence of chlamydeous, a bacterial STD that causes infertility, is several times higher in Iran than in Western countries. Former president Mahmoud Ahmadinejad began campaigning for earlier marriage and bigger families in 2009, but fertility has continued to fall.

Take for instance, John Kerry, in his latest attempt to mediate peace between Israel and the Palestinians, who decried Israel's economic prosperity as "momentary" and "illusionary". Though the State Department later said Kerry was merely describing a development that he opposed, the true import of his comment was clear. The secretary was issuing an implicit threat to Israel that if it failed to give in to his demands, it would be isolated and its goods subject to economic blockade. Those are the words of a bully determined to pressure the Jewish state to give in to demands that would gravely weaken its security and its economy.

Given the situation as described, the question remains then, why does the Israeli government fall into various diplomatic initiatives and not reject those attempts and ignore the two state solution and insist on a one state solution.

I will try to explain this phenomenon. Israel's public debt is now at a reasonable level, having been reduced from 275% of GDP in the 1980 to 70-80% of GDP more recently. Never the less the Israeli economy has been running in deficit throughout her existence. In order to cover their deficit, Israel needs to borrow money in the international markets. To do so, they are relying on the USA to get loan guarantees with low interest rates.

After using up the foreign exchange reserves backing the currency, as required by the British mandatory system, Israel embarked on a continuous search for foreign resources: Institutional transfers, U.S. loans and grants, German Reparations and Restitutions, private transfers, State of Israel Bonds, and other foreign loans and private investment.

The subject of economic dependence has been of great concern and widely debated throughout Israel's history. In the first decades, the main issue was Israel's reliance on an import surplus and the need to mobilize unilateral transfers and foreign loans to finance it. Expectations were that Israel would not be able to continue to mobilize sufficient funds to maintain such a large surplus. The criterion for measuring economic dependence was the share of this import surplus in Israel's total resources, or a variant, its size relative to the GDP. This ratio was, in real terms, as high as 20 percent, particularly following crisis periods. However, in recent years, as exports grew faster than imports, Israel eliminated the import surplus problem.

A different cause for concern, which gives the term "economic dependence" a derogatory implication, has been that the domestic economy is subject to outside influences, which can be used to exert political pressure. In the early decades, much of the financing of the import surplus came from two sources, Germany (as a result of the Reparations) and the U.S. With the decline of the import surplus, this aspect of dependence became relatively less important, but many were troubled by what they considered over reliance of the economy on U.S. aid, quite apart from U.S. political influence.

U.S. economic assistance to Israel has taken many forms over the years. The first U.S. aid was the loan from the Export-Import Bank in

1949, which was of crucial importance, not only as a source of funds, but also as a vote of confidence in the Israel economy. There after, even though U.S. aid provided a significant share of capital inflow, its composition, rather than its size, has been the cause for concern.

U.S. aid has been mainly in the form of economic grants and military loans and grants. Economic grants commenced in 1972, and continued until 2008. Some military loans were received from 1959, but substantial loans were given in 1971 and continued until 1984. Military grants commenced in 1974 and have grown substantially, especially since the decision to phase out economic aid. The total of all U.S. aid, over a sixty-year period, amounted to over $100 billion.

The 10-year military aid agreement adopted in 2007 called for gradually increasing annual military grants from the $2.4 billion in 2008 to $3.15 billion by 2013 and to remain at that level through 2018. This was an important contribution to Israel's defense budget - in 2008 the military aid constituted some 18 percent – and was equal to about 1.3 percent of Israel's GDP. Thus, the present and promised future levels of U.S. direct financial aid, all for military purposes, are clearly of significant monetary benefit. However, the economy could function without this financial aid, if deemed politically necessary. But the reliance on the U.S. for military equipment, which cannot be found elsewhere, regardless of whether or not the U.S. finances it, is an indicator of economic dependence.

The recent financial crisis, starting in the U.S., was quickly transmitted to the rest of the world. Israel was fortunate in that its banking community was not strongly affected, but the downturn in the world economy had its effect, creating a temporary recession in Israel as well. Precisely, this is because Israel has been so successful in becoming an open economy with its exports - in particular the high-tech industries.

With major engines for its economic growth, it has become vulnerable to fluctuations in the global economy. It may be argued that, in this sense, Israel is no different from all other economies integrated into the global economy. But adding to this more general aspect of "dependence", Israel's reliance on U.S. military assistance leads to the conclusion that Israel today is far from economically independent. Furthermore, any contribution to Israel is tax deductible and this can be easily reversed. Without spare parts, for their air force, the entire fleet would be grounded.

All presidents of the USA are well aware of this dependency and use it frequently to pressure Israel to concede to the Arabs. This was done to Israel in Sinai, which Israel evacuated three times, in 1948, 1956, and in 1981. Even today, Jimmy Carter openly threatened Begin to do so in the Camp David negotiations with Sadat of Egypt in 1979.

The chief assistant, to Secretary of State John Kerry, indicated to the Israeli politicians that if you are dependent on the USA, you have to do as they say. He is right, however, this situation forces Israel to stay in a state of limbo without being able to solve their dispute with the Arabs and, slowly but surely, put upon themselves political threats from the international communities of BDS and many others. In the meantime, the Jews around the world, with a leading journalist Thomas Friedman, organize as lobbyists to pressure Israel "for its own welfare" to listen to what the USA advises. By Israel dragging the two states solution without an end, even the Scandinavians countries, which were friendly to Israel, started to become anti-Israeli. Napoleon once said "Only stupid people learn from their own experience" the Israeli political leadership doesn't even learn from their own experience, they have to stop this sitcom of policy with the Palestinian and follow a rigid consistent, regardless of their economic reversals, policy as follow:
I should begin by noting the obvious: it is very hard to write about the Arab-Israeli conflict without being drawn into the solutions sweepstakes. In one way or another, once you confront the issues, you're expected to offer a solution to them or at least to embrace one out of the several already publicly available. What are needed are changes to the Israeli mindset—a mindset for which we Israelis have

paid a harsh price—I can't avoid pointing to a few practical instances of a way forward.

I'm advocating: "A single, Jewish state west of the Jordan with a fairly accommodated Arab minority. This version of a "one-state" solution is as much a fantasy as the "two-state" solution that is a non-starter. To many this poses two problems. The first is the "long-standing international consensus in favor of an independent Palestinian state," which ensures that any Israeli effort to annex the West Bank would be intolerable to world opinion and result not only in harsh economic sanctions but also, in diplomatic and political isolation. The second is the so-called "demographic problem": granting citizenship to so many Arabs, they claim, would threaten Israel's Jewish identity and conferring any other political or legal status on them would be morally repugnant.

Instead of either a one-state or a two-state solution, they put forth their own proposal: a confederation, in which the whole territory would be divided in terms of sovereignty, thus allowing the majority in each state to retain its national identity, but would remain a single geographic entity with freedom of travel, labor, and residence for all.
This idea, which they call "two-states-minus," is better than any other two-state option, and it rests on sound reasoning. Unfortunately, it strikes me as even more fantastic than mine. I don't believe that one small territory can hold these two national movements. In my view, it would be easier to restore Palestinians to their

former status as "plain" Arabs—and I'm not saying that would be easy, either—than to re-direct Palestinian nationalism into some sort of cooperative political arrangement with Israel.

In any case, however, it would be possible to craft a model of governance that would benefit all parties. But, to repeat, I never meant that this would be simple or easy to do. The issues are both extremely complicated and of long standing and any future effort to address them, within my proposed framework, would necessarily require both a great deal of time and uncommon amounts of creativity. Nevertheless, had Israel invested in "my" option but a fraction of the effort poured into the futile Oslo process, we would likely have already come up with a number of elegant and inventive approaches to the problems it raises.

My point here is a general one, worth dwelling on for another moment. My writing wasn't intended as a political action item. Instead, I tried to outline a positive vision, to suggest a wider horizon. I firmly believe that adopting such a vision would lead to a better future for my countrymen and also for the Palestinian Arabs.

Thus, many in the international community are somehow convinced that the Israeli presence in the West Bank is illegal, as if a Palestinian state existed there before 1967 and therefore the land is "occupied." They are wrong, but somebody needs to say and to show that they are wrong: to say it and show it consistently, steadily, and tirelessly until the message is absorbed and accepted by those with the capability of moving the needle of world opinion.

Unfortunately, how the world thinks is very much connected with the way Israelis think, and connected especially with their own lack of confidence in their claim to the land. Their current mindset is the combined fruit of international acceptance of Arab propaganda and a homegrown failure of nerve. Here's a typical example: when accused by the international court in the Hague of building its security fence on Palestinian land, Israel declined to correct the misconception. In fact the land isn't Palestinian; indeed, under international law, Israel has the best claim to it. But instead of making that argument, Israel claimed only a "security need" to confiscate land for the fence. Unsurprisingly, the court condemned it.

Adopting a different position and sticking to it would not be the work of a year or two. From today's perspective, the task of placing a new concept of justice on the international agenda seems little short of a mission impossible. But the effort must be made, if for no other reason than that all other solutions are recipes for continued war and rejectionism. Waiting for Arab acceptance is a long-term exercise; trying to negotiate with Arab *non*-acceptance only makes it longer.

As for the demographic challenge, here too, I have no simple solution, but the threat may not be as dire as some choose to believe. Recent analyses suggest that trends in birth rates are working in favor of the Jews, not the Arabs. Adding an option of free emigration and the possibility of Jordanian citizenship, one might achieve a net result of a reasonable number of new Israeli Arab citizens, people who have chosen to be part of the Jewish state and don't want to undermine it.

As I continue to insist, the main factor is Arab rejectionism. If we Israelis are patient enough and determined enough to overcome it, the Middle East equation could acquire a totally new look. Issues now unsolvable would yield to reasonable compromise, and rejectionism would be replaced by a notion of the common good. Is this a fantasy? In terms of the present situation, yes. But there's no reason to think the present situation must last forever, and even less reason to set it in stone.

 The Arab non-acceptance is a permanent condition." Unfortunately, people see this as totally unrealistic. If we ask the Christian Arabs living in the West Bank village of Tayibe why

178

they can't or won't bring themselves to cooperate with the Jews of nearby Ofra, then how can we even think of any large-scale acceptance?

My answer is simple: there is nothing deep about the refusal or reluctance of the Tayibe villagers to cooperate. Their rejectionism is a function of politics, of attitudes introduced as part and parcel of Palestinian nationalist propaganda and before that of pan-Arab propaganda—and, of Israel's tacit acquiescence in that propaganda. The villagers' attitudes, too, can change and changing Israeli attitudes will help change theirs as well.

Sometimes, dynamic thinking reveals possibilities nobody has noticed or dared to acknowledge. A Frenchman who spoke in the EU agency office in Jerusalem, whose main mission is to deliver EU aid to Gaza, was serenely convinced that Israel—which had long since left the territory—was still acting the role of evil oppressor, exercising its malignant power by obstructing the shipment of goods to the Gazan people. When pointed out that since Gaza was overpopulated, and since most of its residents were not locals but uprooted refugees, a better way to improve their lot would be to facilitate their move to countries willing to absorb them. According to surveys, 40 percent of Gazans said they would be happy to leave. Why not help them?

His reply was startling in its candor. "Are you kidding? 40 percent? It's probably 99 percent. *All* of them want to leave!" Well, we repeated, have you thought of helping them? "No. Never." Why not? "Because if they leave, it'd be like releasing Israel from its responsibility for the *nakba*." So—we tried again—you want to keep them there for the sake of a political vendetta. What if Israel admitted its responsibility, and agreed to compensate not only the refugees, but also their grandchildren?

Our questions were too much for him; he had nothing to reply. So trapped by propaganda was this sincere and pleasant European as to be unable to think of the good of the people he was charged with supporting, let alone the future good of the neighborhood.

Do I believe Benjamin Netanyahu would actually be prepared to ignite a political war with the American administration and world opinion by pushing for a one-state solution? Practically speaking: no, I don't think so even though Netanyahu has already come close to doing precisely that over the issue of the Iranian nuclear threat. In the long run, things do change, sometimes radically, and some of these changes will be the late-blooming results of shifts in people's way of thinking now.

We have to do something about UNRWA and the refugee camps in which generations of Palestinian Arabs have been effectively held captive. We need to mobilize support in the U.S. Congress for changing UNRWA's mandate. Some progress was made; the effort continues, and it should be bolstered.

Last but not least, today's Israelis show a lack of confidence in their national project, but in technological and scientific innovation, in particular, today's Israelis are a marvelously spirited bunch. This has greatly contributed to increased prosperity and well being.
But this undoubted success has nothing to do

with Israeli feelings about the conflict with the

Palestinians, an issue over which Israeli

society suffers from deep self-doubt—so deep

as to raise questions about its own sense of

National legitimacy.

This is especially true among the ranks of the older elites. *My Promised Land: The Triumph and the Tragedy of Israel*, the recent best-seller by Ari Shavit—who is considered a mainstream Zionist—exemplifies the effects of this debilitating condition, as both Ruth Wisse in Mosaic **and Sol Stern in** *The Daily Beast* have acutely pointed out. Even that supposed warmonger, Ariel Sharon, in his last years, referred to Israelis as "conquerors" in their own land. Self-doubt doesn't go much deeper than that.

While I opposed the Oslo Accord that, at least in conception, was not "so irredeemably foolish as to impugn the mental faculties of its proponents." It might be right about that, but, I remember vividly the warnings of Oslo's opponents—precise, well founded, crystal clear, and comprehensively argued, but falling on deaf ears in the euphoria promoted by Oslo's prophets and promoters.

Important to mention in this context is that, prior to Oslo, Israel consistently deemed the Palestinian national movement to be beyond legitimacy. Negotiating with that terrorist movement, or even meeting its officials, was illegal; so was displaying the Palestinian flag. All of this vanished in the sweeping thrill of imminent reconciliation that turned yesterday's lawbreakers into today's peacemakers. This was not rational; it was an irrational attempt, born of reckless impatience, to escape reality—and it entailed the abandonment of any search for a genuine peace. The day afterward, systematic, murderous Arab terror, on a here to fore unprecedented scale, spread across the country.

High-tech ventures are nice, but in the diplomatic and political arena, Israel has been conducting itself in survival mode, not in confidence mode. If the country is under so much international pressure today, that is at least partly the result of decades of willed silence, amounting to impotence, in the face of the arrantly false and defamatory Palestinian "narrative."

David Ben-Gurion once famously remarked that, in the end, "what the Jews do" is more important than "what the Gentiles say" (or think). As many commentators have noted, not everything depends on us; but much does. And what doesn't depend on us is a challenge we have to face and do everything in our power to overcome.

Now that the Israeli-Palestinian peace negotiations have ended in failure. Many suggest taking advantage of the political limbo to advance the above unilateral plans, however the USA foreign policies failures in Syria, Nigeria, Ukraine, Egypt and the rest of the world it will never stop pressing Israel back to the negotiating table with the Palestinians. It is imperative that the Israeli government should reverse the Oslo Accord and annex Area C that was given to the PLO.

Epilogue

As time passes and current events change world developments, it is the nature of the well-meaning human memory to rid itself of superfluous views. People retain only what in their view has proven to be most important in the light of later events, especially when they are subjected to a barrage of criticism from the mass media. Yet this is also the weak side of memory. Being biased, it cannot help adjusting past reality to fit present needs and future hopes. When it comes to Israel, this weakness persists further because of the unrelenting and virulent hatred of the Arabs. This has caused Israel to lose its compass.

Almost 60 years have passed since the establishment of the State of Israel. The novelty of a Jewish state has long since worn off. The world has become accustomed to its existence, and memory of the reasons for its creation is fading; the world is a far different place with different problems and different concerns from those with which it was preoccupied immediately following World War II. Ironic as it may be, the Arab-Israeli conflict has remained unchanged since 1948. Furthermore, Israel has remained as vulnerable as it was in 1948. This is the essence of my book.

Charles Darwin in his famous book *On the Origin of Species* observed an intriguing phenomenon among the marine iguana in the Galapagos Islands. The space in which the female lays her eggs is very limited and thus fiercely contested by other females. The female first shows a maternal instinct in protecting her own brood of eggs with extreme tenacity; however, once she succeeds in chasing away her rivals, she walks away without ever checking whether or not a later rival has appeared and destroyed her eggs. It is as if she is more concerned with winning a battle than with protecting her offspring, which are her future. Israel resembles the marine iguana. Generations of dedicated and brave Jews sacrificed their time and frequently their lives for the establishment of their own state, but now that it has been established they are ready to walk away.

The Arab-Israeli dispute is a very simple one to explain. The Arabs see Israel as an entity that is wedged into a region they consider to be their own. The Jews immigrated to Palestine when the region was part of the Ottoman Empire, without any eviction of the indigenous population. This occurred in the same way many Arabs migrated to the area from various other parts of the Middle East. Any military defeat at the hands of Israel increases the Arabs' resolve to uproot this "foreign body" from the area. The Arabs with their demographic advantage and huge oil resources can afford to be patient, since time is on their side. To the West, the Arabs can play the Palestinian card for a long time, each time increasing demands to increase the number of Palestinian refugees to be settled in Israel. Furthermore, culturally they are too far from being assimilated into the Western world to change their attitude toward the West and Israel. It should be clear that the way to solve the Arab-Israeli dispute is not through concession. The slogan of "territory for peace" can be applied only to its absolute limit.

Israel, on the other hand, possesses all the ideals that the United States claims to promote in the world. Israel is a Jeffersonian democracy, a Westernized enlightened society guided by human rights and social welfare principles. Unlike the clerical Arab regimes that are a breeding ground for global terrorism, Israel is a beacon of modernity that tolerates openness of society and ideas and will never support any terrorism that poses a threat to the world. All this does not provide Israel any comfort since realpolitik dictates that the United States and Western Europe ignore Israel and support the Arabs; after all, oil is thicker than Jewish blood. Based on this, it is clear that Israel cannot throw itself on U.S. mercy, since the U.S. support is unreliable and its duration is not guaranteed. Therefore, Israel has to be able to withstand any pressures that will compromise its future existence. This requires the polity of Israel to be dedicated and innovative in order to promote its ability to act as a strong, responsible, international player, unyielding to the Arabs, that can back up its positions with (a) leverage, (b) cohesion, and (c) clarity of purpose. Only a leadership that can mobilize all the resources at its disposal—economic, military, diplomatic, and media—can do this. What we see instead is a government by cronyism with ever-increasing dependency on the U.S. dollar. Israel is unable, by itself, to regain its pre-statehood tenacity.

The Israelis rushed to achieve normalcy once the state was established. A further boost, in their make-believe world, occurred after their victory in the Six-Day War of 1967. This brought them the euphoric sensation that they were invincible and secure in the Middle East. By the time the Yom Kippur War erupted, the rude awakening had turned into desperation and a sense of resignation. The phenomenon of power self-preservation revealed itself in its full force. Most of the upper echelon of the pre-statehood society converted from a pioneering, dedicated, unselfish, patriotic, goal-oriented group of people into material gatherers and corporate entrepreneur achievers. Even the military institution became politicized and turned into another form of career advancement with all the associated perks. The pre-statehood leaders' creativity that had shown their ability to see the long-range problems, and provided ways to solve them, vanished. They were replaced by various academic institutions that produced ample amounts of data and studies on various current issues, similar to the ones published in the United States, with the full intention of achieving publication in the United States. This provides the small-minded politicians who are in charge of the country the basis for their longevity in power by diverting the public at large from debating the real issues facing them. Israel cannot afford to emulate the United States without the financial support from the outside. With the Cold War gone and the United States embarking on a mission of flexing its muscles throughout the world, almost unmolested, Israel can no longer assume any strategic importance to the United States in its quest to build various coalitions. Israel's existence has become important only to its own citizens and to the Jewish community throughout the world. Israel should face reality and ask itself how long the financial aid will flow once its territorial concessions end and the "final peace" is achieved according to the international community.

Most of what I have written here is not new. Most of these facts have been mentioned in other publications, among the most distinguished the magazine *Commentary,* by FLAME (Facts and Logic About the Middle East), in *Near East Report,* and by many syndicated columnists. All of these writers deal with the defense of the Jewish state in order to expose false statements and interpretations in the media and the diplomatic world. They are all eager to inform their readers of the possibility of harm to Israel and its allies as a result of the pursuit of a specific policy. However, none of them explain why we have a complete paralysis of Israel's stewardship in pursuing their advice. They are consistently oblivious to the fact that Israel is ignoring their advice, which defies logic, because it is facing ever-increasing U.S. financial support that "obligates" it to ignore the logic. Many of those in the U.S. Congress and people formerly or currently in U.S. government positions, such as

Jean Kirkpatrick and even Donald Rumsfeld, are able to articulate what Israel's position ought to be vis-à-vis the Arabs far better than anyone in Israel.

Even when the U.S. Congress adopted a resolution to move the U.S. embassy to Jerusalem, it was the Israeli officials who urged them to reverse it in order to abide by the U.S. State Department's policy of minimizing the Arab hostility while conducting the "peace process." The *Commentary* writers refuse to proclaim the real cause behind Israel's misguided behavior, which is based on total subservience to the U.S. wishes. The *Commentary* writers still insist on providing Israel with a platform, full of detailed policy guidelines, to follow in order to address its problems with the Arabs. They fail to see, whether through their wishful thinking or simple naiveté, that Israel never issued a proposal of its own. They still prefer to view the U.S. policies imposed on Israel as a part of "Israel's own policies," and they proceed to blame the lack of a solution on simple policy errors that stem from ideological points of view.

These writers are continuously coming up with new "road maps" and policy agendas for Israel to implement and adopt. They ignore the fact that the public in Israel ceased to make any proposals after the Madrid Conference in 1991 and that it trusts any solution to U.S. decision makers. They ignore what happened in the Camp David negotiations between Egypt and Israel in 1978 when Begin and his entourage tried to save some of the territories in Sinai from being relinquished to Egypt. They ignore the fact that President Carter threatened to cut aid to Israel. As a result of his threat, Israel not only returned the entire Sinai to Egypt but also agreed to provide self-determination to the Palestinians. They ignore the fact that Secretary James Baker, in his testimony before Congress, gave Itzchak Shamir his phone number, telling him to call when he was ready to talk about peace with the Palestinians. This was a great insult in the context of diplomatic affairs, reflecting how much respect Israel is given by the United States. These writers ignore the fact that the Israelis failed to gain the release of Jonathan Pollard from a U.S. prison. They ignore the fact that Ariel Sharon had to get permission from the United States to arrest or deport Yassir Arafat and could not declare an end to the Oslo Accords. How can one expect Israel to "disobey" Bush's "road map" after its historical diplomatic behavior? Perhaps by neglecting to acknowledge these facts, the *Commentary* writers can avoid the need for any personal character attacks on the Israeli leaders and stay within the norm of the unwritten code of ethics. Only the Canadians can call George Bush a moron, regardless of how many people would offer their agreement with this statement, myself not included.

Israel has reached its lowest point of capitulating to the United States and the international community by refusing to come up with any proposals of its own for ending the Palestinian impasse in order to avoid antagonizing President Bush. The Sharon government has hoped for time to change Bush's "road map" by advancing 100 reservations. At the same time, the Labor party opposition has "urged" President Bush to implement his "road map" even before dealing with Iraq. The Labor party even calls for an international mandate to be sustained by a multinational force. This force is not only to supervise reform of the Palestinian system and the disarmament of the militias, but also to monitor the evacuation of territories in order to impose a strict and binding peace plan. In either case, both the government of Israel and the opposition are throwing their destiny into the hands of the Arabs, who will never recognize Israel, and the international community that always supports the Arab point of view and cares less if Israel one day disappears. If they do not know, Bush's "road map" is nothing more than the Saudi proposal that would force Israel to its pre-June 1967 borders, with the inclusion of a Palestinian state. This is already established by the promise President Bush gave to the Saudis for their support of U.S. actions against Iraq. If this level of capitulation does not cause consternation among Israel's supporters, I do not know what could.

What is even more disturbing is the illusion within the Israeli polity that Israel is a sovereign country that is master and in full control of its own destiny and not a bystanding and passive entity. Between September 1993 and September 2000, we witnessed a historical experiment, the Oslo Accords, that were intended to negotiate a final resolution of the decades-old conflict between Israelis and Palestinians. This accord came to a standstill with the collapse of the Camp David summit in July 2000. Soon thereafter the Palestinian opted to launch a war, which they call Intifada II.

All the pundits were stunned by the collapse of the security arrangements that were at the heart of the Oslo Accords. After all, the people who negotiated the Oslo Accords were from of a generation of experienced, professional, security specialists—many of them battle-hardened veterans. Yet they failed to see the possibility that the Oslo Accords could be exploited by the Palestinians as a platform of war and rather than serving as a basis for peace.

As if the Palestinian popular uprising from December 1987 to September 1993, Intifada I, that by all accounts allowed the Palestinians to operate in a terror-based war while limiting and restricting Israel's options to respond, resulted in the Palestinian "defeat." The pundits convinced themselves, with a heavy dose of self-illusion and wishful thinking, that the Oslo Accords were a panacea, that the "defeated" Palestinians would live up to the security arrangements outlined in Oslo. It never occurred to those so-called experts that the Oslo Accords were initiated precisely because Israel was defeated and could not sustain Intifada I. The Arabs had finally found a method by which they could not only defeat Israel but also discredit it in the eyes of the entire world, including its own Jewish population. Why should they give up a good thing? For them the Oslo Accords were simply intended to revive the PLO after their eviction from Lebanon and legitimize their infrastructure present in the West Bank and Gaza Strip. They knew full well that Israel could never reverse its policy, simply because the White House would not "permit "it.

That Intifada II replaced the stone-throwing Palestinian mob with live ammunition and even heavy weapons, as well as a command structure of PLO battle-hardened veterans who are receiving their supply from Israel's "peace" partners, Egypt and Jordan—all of this is thanks to the Oslo Accords, and it is still limiting and restricting Israel's options to respond. This, plus the fact that Israel still does not renounce the Oslo Accords and allows the PLO to operate in the West Bank with impunity, can mean one thing and one thing only. Israel is not a sovereign country that controls its own destiny.

However, no matter how perplexing the situation may be, politicians and academics alike cling to the notion that Israel is in control of its own political situation; and many of them, well-meaning and peace-loving people, are getting involved in the Geneva track-two effort to negotiate an Israeli-Palestinian permanent status agreement, which is largely based on the 1993 Oslo agreement. At the same time, less glaring examples of blindness appear in ever-increasing numbers of Israeli think tanks, hard at work in providing agendas and outlines that Israel ought to abide by in order to achieve security and peace. Similarly to the *Flame* and *Commentary* writers, none of these observers ever suggest that a prerequisite to implementation of any agenda is a complete overhaul of Israel's polity. No politician will ever accept the notion that he or she is irrelevant and useless when it comes to foreign and security policy. The writers are resigned to the dictum expressed by Upton Sinclair regarding journalists in general—"It is difficult to get a man to understand something when his salary depends upon his not understanding." Furthermore, demanding an overhaul of Israel's polity would reduce the publication of articles dealing with the Israeli-Arab conflict and certainly would eliminate some of the think tanks. Perhaps all these are underlying causes for avoiding reality.

The Arab-Israeli dispute should be viewed in comparison to the Cold War and not as one between two nations competing for the same real estate, that is, the Jews and the Palestinians. The boundaries between Israel and the Arab states were drawn in 1949 under the UN-sponsored cease-fire agreement. In a similar case, the Cold War was based on the borders between the Soviet Union empire and the West as a result of the Second World War. In contrast to the situation in the Arab-Israeli dispute, the two sides in the Cold War had full diplomatic relations. The United States, as the leader of the West, did not lose sight of the core of the dispute and fought to contain the Soviet Union by preventing any of its attempts to expand its empire. There were some glitches in U.S. policy, such as Vietnam, Ethiopia, Afghanistan, and Cuba. Although the "lesson of Munich" dominated Cold War thinking, it did not always guide events in the periphery. One thing was clear in the Cold War; the Soviet Union was intent on expanding its empire by means of guerrilla warfare of national liberation or by sheer military invasion. What is most important to remember about the Cold War is that at its core the containment had to be clear and foolproof, without any territorial concessions. The United States understood that any territorial concession would only invite increased aggression, the "lesson of Munich."

The same conditions exist in the Arab-Israeli dispute with few exceptions. The Arab countries, like the Soviet Union versus the West, are set on destroying Israel; but since the Arabs refused to sign any peace accord prior to 1967, the borders were fluid and subject to change in case of aggression by the Arabs. Israel acted like the West, which during the Cold War was not involved in undermining the Soviet empire and refused to intervene in the Hungarian revolt in 1956 and the Czechoslovakia uprising of 1968. Therefore, the new borders of Israel after the 1967 war were legal and legitimate under any international law. The "lesson of Munich" should have applied here as well.

As the United States was prepared for confrontation with Nazi Germany and with the Soviet Union and global terrorism, so Israel has to be resolved to fight the Arabs. For both the United States and Israel, this tests their strength, character, and endurance. For the United States, the issue is preservation of the free world; for Israel the issue is its own preservation. No country should have the moral right to demand from Israel any concessions that it would refuse to make itself under far more favorable circumstances. This high moral calling should be drilled daily into the media elite in both America and Europe that presently calls for negotiating a settlement with the Palestinians by removing the Jewish settlements and withdrawing from the "occupied" territories. This display of leavened platitudes should be stopped. Napoleon said, "Only stupid people learn from their own experience." It is time to apply the lessons from the Second World War and the Cold War as well. How would Napoleon characterize people who do not learn even from their own experience? For Israel it is decision time—"to be or not to be."

Conclusion

1. The Arabs initiated the Arab-Israeli wars as a joint policy. Therefore, the Arabs should jointly be held responsible for the negative consequences of those wars, including the loss of territory, as well as the Palestinian refugee problem. Israel is continuously in a defensive posture while the Arabs have no motivation to solve the dispute. So far, we can conclude that the Arabs have not given up their dream of eradicating Israel, even if it takes a long time.

2. There has been a failure of political leadership in Israel, involving the lack of a clear strategic vision about Israel's borders and its long-term relationship with its Arab neighbors.

3. That failure of leadership has resulted in Israel's giving back territories gained in the wars without gaining long-term peace with its neighbors. Israel needs to develop a proper national strategic vision articulated through a coherent foreign ministry.

4. Israel's economic and political relationship with the United States creates a dependency that weakens Israel.

5. Arab nations leverage their oil resources and the U.S. dependency on those

resources to push the United States into applying pressure on Israel. The United States extorts concessions from Israel and thereby gains in peaceful negotiations what the Arabs could not win on the battlefield, namely the destruction of Israel.

6. Due to the U.S. dependence on Arab oil and Israel's lack of natural resources, the United States cannot apply pressure on the Arabs to seek a real lasting peace. However, due to Israel's dependence on U.S. economic and military aid, the United States can and does apply pressure on Israel in any negotiations involving the Arabs.

7. The solution is, first, for Israel to wean itself from its economic dependency on the United States, and secondly to vigorously pursue military solutions to Palestinian/Arab terrorism, citing its survival as justification.

8. And finally, it defies logic for Israel to build a security wall and establish a Palestinian state.

Bibliography

Avineri, Shlomo, *Moses Hess: Prophet of Communism and Zionism,* New York University Press, New York, 1985.

Azkin, Benjamin, *States and Nations,* Doubleday Anchor, New York, 1966.

Barnet, Richard, *Roots of War,* Atheneum, New York, 1972.

Biale, David, *Power and Powerlessness in Jewish History,* Shocken Books, 1986.

Borochov, Ber, *Class Struggle and the Jewish Nation,* Transaction Books, New Brunswick, New Jersey, 1984.

Bulloch, John, and Morris, Harvey, *No Friends but the Mountains,* Oxford University Press, New York, 1992.

Elam, Yigal, *An Introduction to Zionist History* [in Hebrew], A. Levin Epstein Limited, Ramat Gan, Israel

Fallaci, Oriana, *The Rage and the Pride,* Rizzoli, New York, 2002.

Friedland, Edward, Seabury, Paul, and Wildavsky, Aaron, *The Great Détente Disaster,* Basic Books, New York, 1975.

Halevi, Nadav, Trade and Economic Dependence.

Harkabi, Yehoshafat, *The Arab Position in Their Conflict with Israel* [in Hebrew], Dvir Company Limited, Tel Aviv, Israel, 1968.

_____, *Israel's Position in Her Conflict with the Arabs* [in Hebrew], Dvir Company Limited, Tel Aviv, Israel, 1970.

_____, *Israel's Fateful Hour,* Harper & Row, New York, 1989.

Herzl, Theodor, *The Jewish State,* Dover Publications, New York, 1988.

Horowitz, Dan, and Lissak, Moshe, *Trouble in Utopia,* State University of New York Press, Albany, 1989.

Kurzman, Dan, *Soldier of Peace: The Life of Yitzhak Rabin 1922-1995,* Harper Collins, New York, 1998.

Laqueur, Walter, and Rubin, Barry, *The Road to Jerusalem,* Macmillan, New York, 1968.

_____, *The Israel-Arab Reader,* Facts On File, New York, 1985.

Lewis, Bernard, *What Went Wrong?,* Oxford University Press, New York, 2002.

Lewis, Charles, *The Buying of the President,* Avon Books, New York, 1996.

Peters, Joan, *From Time Immemorial,* Harper & Row, New York, 1984.

Pryce-Jones, David, *The Closed Circle,* Harper Perennial, New York, 1989.

Schueftan, Dan, *A Jordanian Option* [in Hebrew], Yad Tabenkin, Israel, 1986.

Sheffer, Gabriel (Editor), *The Big Powers and the October 1973 War,* Van Leer Jerusalem Foundation, Jerusalem, Israel, 1975.

Zohar, Ezra, *Sodom or Helem* [in Hebrew], Dvir-Publishers, Tel Aviv, Israel, 1987.

_____, *A Concubine in the Middle East* [in Hebrew], Dvir-Publishers, Tel Aviv, Israel, 1994.